Beetles, Bugs and Butterflies

A CROCHET STORY OF TINY
CREATURES AND BIG DREAMS

Lydia Tresselt

www.sewandso.co.uk

CONTENTS

WELCOME TO LALYLALAND

HELLO BUG LOVERS AND CROCHET ADVENTURERS

Grab your research equipment (magnifying glass, flask of tea, crochet hook, scissors and yarn) and follow me into a world full of magic and science, a microcosm of tiny creatures and big dreams!

In this book you will find not only a charming selection of formulas to create scrabbling beetles, beautiful bugs and fluttering butterfly crochet amigurumi, but also a wonderful story to read out loud and ponder on – a tale about growing up, accepting change and the power of dreams.

Watch tiny creatures hatching from their eggs, look on as they munch through a green world, and be astonished at their marvellous transformations when they finally slip out of their cocoons. Along the way, find out why snails are in a hurry, what beetles dream of and what a fly did to get famous.

But the transformations needn't stop there. Use the patterns in this book to create new outfits for your little insect friends. Give your caterpillar a new set of wings for every day of the week, or cover your beetle in the most colourful wing suits. Be inspired by nature to make creatures of your own creation. It's a great little world full of possibilities.

I wish you a lot of fun on your journey of discovery and learning.

Lydia

lalylala expedition leader

LIFE CYCLE OF A BUTTERFLY

THE MAGIC OF COMPLETE METAMORPHOSIS

EGG

BUTTERFLY

CATERPILLAR (LARVA)

COCOON (PUPA)

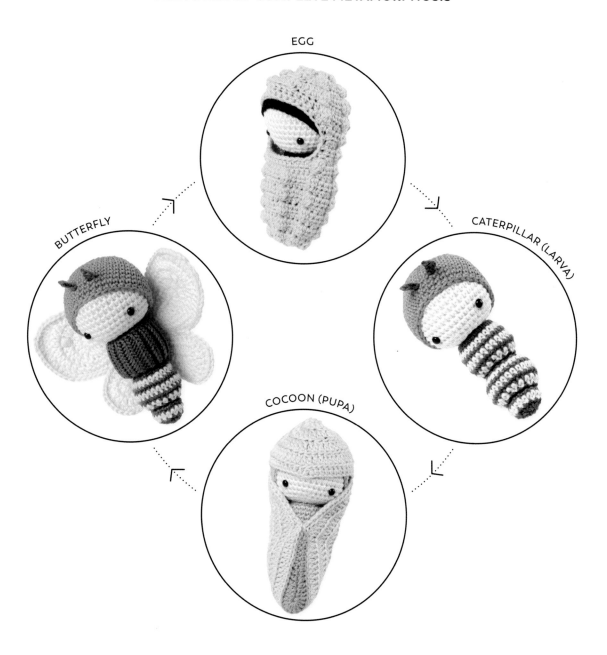

A STORY OF
TINY CREATURES
AND BIG DREAMS

A **CATERPILLAR** wakes up and finds herself in a strange new world. It's round and dark, quite narrow and very boring.

She stays curled up in a ball for a while, but soon she needs to have a good stretch.

Quite suddenly the caterpillar's world bursts open.

"Wow!" she cries with delight. "The world isn't a sphere after all – it's a disc!"

"A green disc, to be precise."

There are more eggs on the disc and
other larvae are hatching out of them.

Everyone introduces themselves and they start to chat about what they want to be when they grow up. They all have grand plans and great expectations!

"What do you want to be, Caterpillar?" one of them asks.

"Oh, umm ... I'm not sure, I haven't decided that yet," she replies bashfully.

While she listens to the others talk about their plans, the caterpillar begins to daydream, absent-mindedly chewing on the edge of the **LEAF**.

A **SNAIL** hatches from one of the eggs. "I'm all grown up already," he says, "I don't want to wait for anyone."

"There's no time to lose," he continues. "I need to start living my life." So, the snail packs his rucksack and heads off straight away.

The larvae stay behind.

The caterpillar is too afraid to follow the quick, brave snail. Quite green with envy, she takes an extra big bite out of the leaf.

A **MAGGOT** hatches from another egg.

"I'll become a famous performer!"
he confidently proclaims.

No-one believes the maggot can do it because he's so small and ugly. But while everyone is still laughing at him, he pupates and the next minute the maggot has turned into a **FLY**!

The fly soars high and dashes here and there. He hums and buzzes whilst performing daring somersaults, surprising everyone with his incredible aerial antics.

After a wild and energetic performance, the fly lands on an exceptionally exotic leaf.

The **VENUS FLYTRAP** closes like the curtain at the end of a show – and then there is silence.

The caterpillar, who has been holding her breath during the fly's exciting performance, slowly exhales. Lost in thought, she takes another bite out of the leaf.

While the other larvae quickly forget about the fly, the caterpillar can't stop thinking about him. She is so fascinated by the flying display that she decides to take a risk too.

The caterpillar has another bite to eat to gather some strength for her bold venture and then concentrates really hard on becoming something different, just like the fly did.

The caterpillar tries so hard that she literally jumps out of her skin!

Disappointed, she sees that although she has become a bit more colourful, she's still just a caterpillar.

"Perhaps I didn't eat enough?" she muses.

The **BEETLE LARVA** thinks that the caterpillar's daydreaming is just a waste of time. "I already know what I want to be," she says. "I have a masterplan!"

"There's no need to rush things like the fly did," the beetle larva decides. First, she'll spend a long time preparing all the details of her future life while she's a larva, then she'll have a short break as a pupa.

And finally she'll get her well-deserved beetle wings, designed with a simple yet elegant pattern.

Compared to the **LADYBIRD**, there's nothing simple or elegant about the caterpillar. Since shedding her skin again, she has become even more wildly coloured.

"Oh dear, why do I just stay the same old, boring caterpillar?" she wonders, sadly.

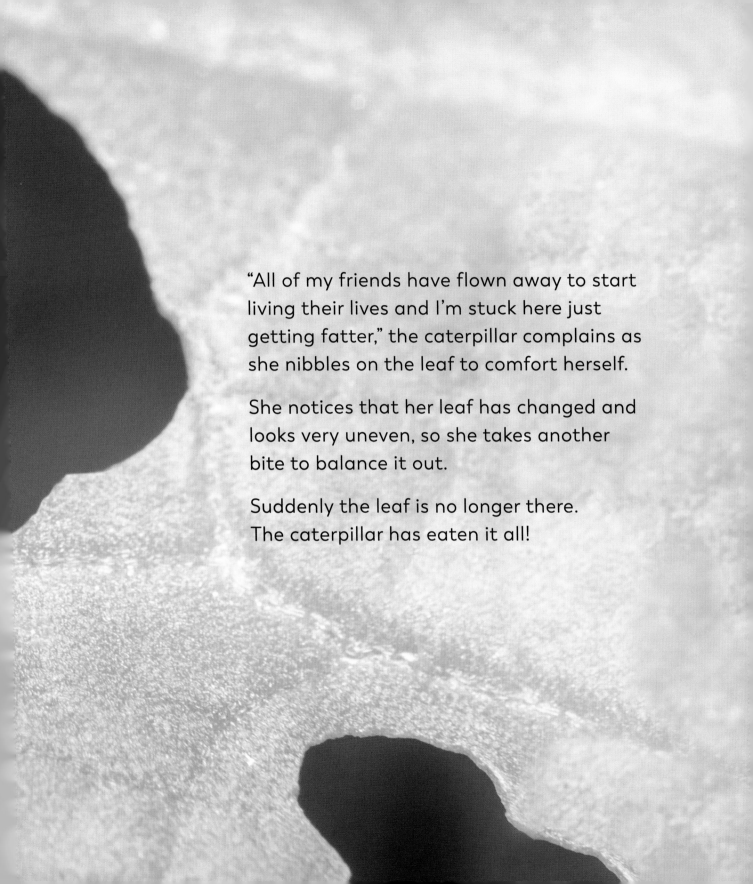

"All of my friends have flown away to start living their lives and I'm stuck here just getting fatter," the caterpillar complains as she nibbles on the leaf to comfort herself.

She notices that her leaf has changed and looks very uneven, so she takes another bite to balance it out.

Suddenly the leaf is no longer there. The caterpillar has eaten it all!

The caterpillar falls and only just manages to hold on to the stem of the leaf. Her life hangs by a silk thread. She is so frightened that she accidentally pupates.

Safe in her cocoon, the caterpillar doesn't stir for a very long time.

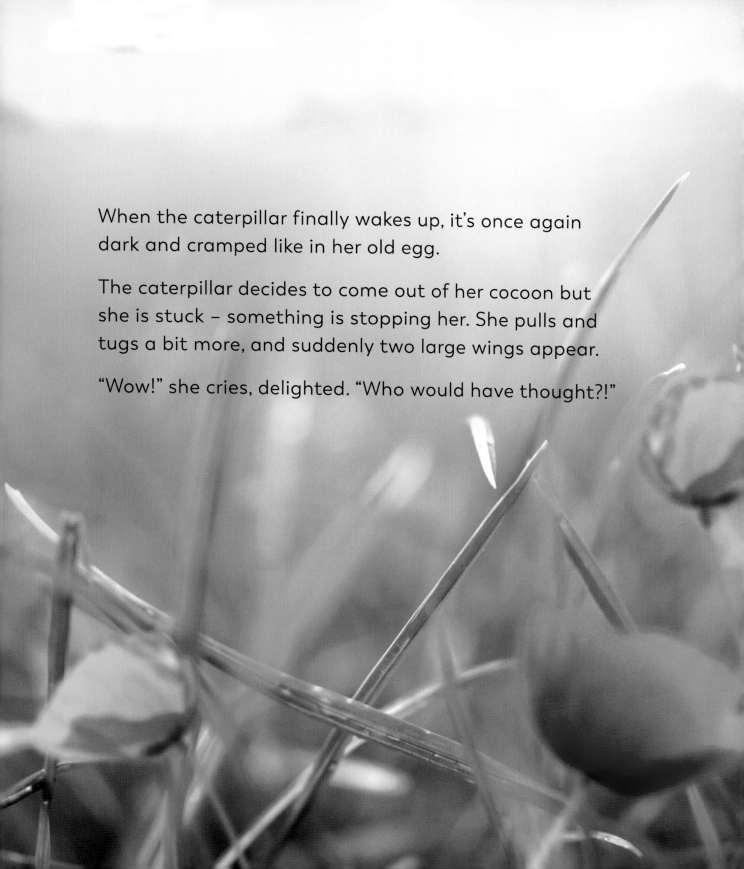

When the caterpillar finally wakes up, it's once again dark and cramped like in her old egg.

The caterpillar decides to come out of her cocoon but she is stuck – something is stopping her. She pulls and tugs a bit more, and suddenly two large wings appear.

"Wow!" she cries, delighted. "Who would have thought?!"

She stays hanging in her cocoon a little while longer to get used to her new wings, and then she's ready to flutter away.

From far above, she sees the small plant where she has lived until now. Then she spots the snail – just a few steps away.

Looking around, she discovers many other plants and **BUTTERFLIES** and, beyond that, a big wide world.

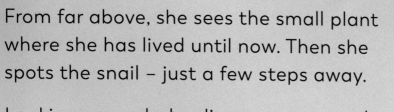

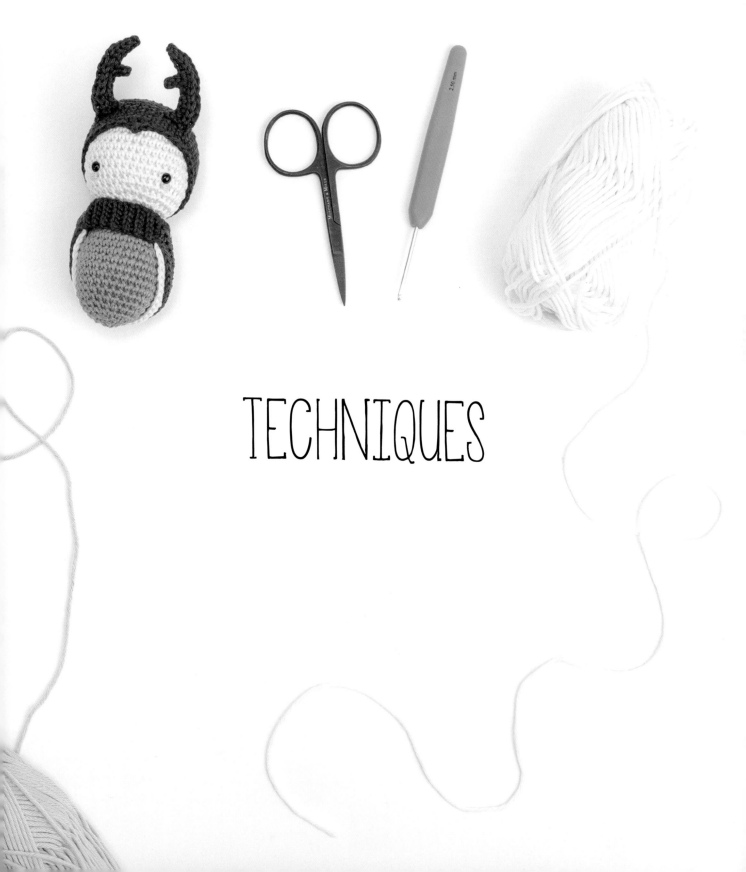

TECHNIQUES

TOOLS & MATERIALS

HOOKS AND YARN

You are free to choose the yarn and hook according to your own personal preference, but you should remember that you may need more than the specified amount of yarn if you choose to crochet your amigurumi from a heavier weight yarn.

Following the original patterns in the book, you will need:

Crochet hook: size US C/2 (2.5mm or 2.25mm) – depending on how tight your crochet stitches are, you could also choose a B/1 (2mm) hook size).

Cotton yarn: sport/4ply (size 2, fine or baby weight).

I used the following yarn by Scheepjes:

Scheepjes Catona (100% Mercerized cotton, 25g/1oz [62m/67yd] or 50g/2oz [125m/137yd], 10 x10cm [5 x 5in] = 26 sts x 36 rows).

Crochet hook: size US E/4 (3.5mm) – you could also choose a G/6 (4mm) hook size.

Cotton yarn: worsted/aran (size 4, medium weight).

I used the following yarn by Scheepjes:

Scheepjes Stone Washed XL (70% cotton/30% acrylic, 50g/2oz [75m/82yd], 10 x10cm [5 x 5in] = 19 sts x 14 rows).

OTHER TOOLS AND MATERIALS

Apart from crochet hooks and yarn, there are a few other things that you'll also need:

Toy safety eyes: black, size 5mm (¼in); alternatively, dark grey yarn to embroider eyes (see safety note).

Beads: 3mm (⅛in) light green for aphid feet and 20mm (¾in) wooden bead for leaf closure (see safety note).

Soft toy stuffing: I used a polyester fibrefill stuffing.

Scissors: pointy and sharp.

Stitch markers: alternatively, use a thread of yarn in a contrast colour, paper clips, or safety pins.

Pins: use glass-headed pins so that they don't get lost inside your amigurumi.

Blunt-tipped yarn/tapestry needle: with an opening big enough to carry your yarn.

Cat slicker brush or soft wire brush: to make the surface of the crochet fabric fuzzy (used for the moth).

GENERAL ADVICE

WORKING THE AMIGURUMI

CHOOSING A HOOK

To prevent your fabric from showing large stretch holes when it's stuffed, choose a smaller hook size than that printed on the ball band of your yarn.

If you crochet rather loosely, choose a smaller hook size as you would do for a standard crochet project.

USING STITCH MARKERS

Mark the first stitch of a round to keep track of where the round begins. This helps when counting your stitches to compare it with the pattern.

STUFFING

To get the right shape for your amigurumi, the most important thing is to stuff it very well. Stuff it as tight as you can – I mean, really tight! When you think that's enough, stuff it a bit more! (You know you've got it right if, when you press your amigurumi, it feels like a tennis ball.) A broken chopstick is the perfect tool to help you to spread the soft stuffing into every little corner.

Rarely a full ball of yarn is needed, so you can make many of the bugs using leftovers from other patterns.

WORKING IN A SPIRAL

For most 3-dimensional parts you will work in a continuous spiral. This means, you won't close each round with a slip stitch into the first stitch of the round, but continue to crochet directly into the first stitch of the previous round to start the next round.

SLIGHTLY MOVING BEGINNING OF THE ROUND

On pieces that are worked in a spiral you will see that the beginning of the round moves slightly to the right (or to the left if you are left-handed) with every finished round. Don't worry about this phenomenon – it's absolutely normal when working in spirals.

WORKING IN CLOSED ROUNDS

Some parts of the amigurumis are worked in closed rounds, which means you will close each round with a slip stitch into the first stitch of the round. The next round starts with one or more initial chain stitches to get the right height for the following stitches and follows the same direction as the previous round. But every rule has its exception and in some patterns you'll be forced to turn the working piece to crochet the next round in the opposite direction, just as you would do if you were working on a flat square, for example.

MODIFYING THE DESIGNS

There are lots of different ways in which you can make your amigurumi unique – here are a few ideas to get you started.

SIZE

Choose a different yarn weight with the corresponding crochet hook size to make a giant or teeny-tiny version.

PURPOSE

You can transform your amigurumi from a toy to something extra special – all you need is imagination.

Turn the caterpillar into a baby rattle by adding a noise-maker into its head.

Make a bigger version of the beetle to place a music box insert into.

Crochet a giant aphid from bulky yarn to use it as a nursery cushion or as a toddler ride-along.

COLOURS

The easiest way to make your amigurumi unique is to change the colours. Use self-striping or colour-changing yarn, or try fuzzy or other textured yarn.

CHARACTER

I prefer my amigurumi with minimum facial expression, but you may wish to add more features. If desired, give your caterpillar a nose and a mouth, or add some yarn hair on her head. To keep your amigurumi looking as kawaii as Japanese candy, place eyes and eyebrows, nose or mouth with care. The eyes, for example, should be placed in the lower third of the head and a nose at almost the same height as the eyes but 1 round down.

EMBROIDERY

Make your amigurumi totally distinctive with surface crochet stitches or embroidery. Pimp up plain crochet fabric with tribal motifs, geometric patterns, flowers, or cross stitch designs. Substitute toy safety eyes with satin stitch circles or work a curving backstitch line for sleepy eyes.

GLITTER AND BLING

To make your amigurumi sparkle, use a metallic effect crochet yarn, or glam it up by using metallic sewing thread or embroidery with your standard crochet yarn (hold both threads together). You can also sew on beads or sequins, but not if the toy is to be given to a child under 3 years of age.

In nature, everything is about diversity, so get inspired!

TERMINOLOGY

NOTE:

The patterns in this book are written using US crochet terms and some of the stitch names differ for the UK, for example single crochet is referred to as double crochet in UK crochet patterns. See the table below for key differences between US and UK crochet terminology.

US	UK
single crochet (sc)	double crochet (dc)
double crochet (dc)	triple crochet (tr)
half double crochet (hdc)	half triple crochet (htr)
triple crochet (tr)	double triple crochet (dtr)

PATTERN ABBREVIATIONS

bl = bobble stitch (see Stitches)

ch = chain stitch

ch1picot/ch2picot = picot stitch (see Stitches)

chsp = chain space

ch-3sp = space under a chain of 3 stitches

ch-2sp = space under a chain of 2 stitches

ch-1sp = space under a chain of 1 stitch

sc2tog = invisible single crochet decrease (crochet together two stitches with a single crochet stitch to lose 1 stitch) (see Tutorials)

dc = double crochet stitch

dc2tog = double crochet decrease (crochet together 2 stitches with a double crochet stitch to lose 1 stitch) (see Tutorials)

hdc = half double crochet stitch

hdc2tog = half double crochet decrease (crochet together 2 stitches with a half double crochet stitch to lose 1 stitch) (see Tutorials)

hdc3tog = half double crochet decrease over 3 stitches (crochet together 3 stitches with a half double crochet stitch to lose 2 stitches)

...-inc = increase (crochet 2 stitches into the same stitch, example: sc-inc, dc-inc, tr-inc)

pm = place marker

sc = single crochet stitch

slst = slip stitch

...blo = work stitch as indicated through back loop only, example: scblo, dcblo, trblo

...flo = work stitch as indicated through front loop only, example: scflo, dcflo, trflo

tr = triple crochet stitch

tr2tog = triple crochet decrease (crochet together 2 stitches with a triple crochet stitch to lose 1 stitch) (see Tutorials)

yo = yarn over (wrap the yarn around the hook)

[...] x times = repeat instructions in brackets as a sequence as many times as written after the closing bracket, example: [...] 5 times

°...° = work instructions between ° and ° all into the same stitch or same spot

(...) = total number of stitches after the row or round (this is placed at the end of the row or round)

KEY TO PATTERN CHARTS

For the butterfly, moth and fly wings, charts have been supplied alongside the written pattern instructions.

◄   **start point**

◁   **start of round/row**

•   **slip stitch**

○   **chain**

+   **single crochet**

T   **half double crochet**

   double crochet

   triple crochet

X X   **single crochet increase**

V   **half double crochet increase**

V   **double crochet increase**

X   **single crochet + half double crochet in same stitch**

V   **half double crochet + double crochet in same stitch**

2)   **ch-2 space**

⌣   **front loop**

⌢   **back loop**

@   **magic loop**

*   **marker**

READING PATTERNS

To follow the patterns, you have to know how to read the instructions, which use abbreviations (see Pattern Abbreviations) and symbols to describe the stitches that have to be done.

[...] X TIMES

You have to repeat all the instructions between the opening and closing bracket as a sequence.

Repeat this sequence as many times as you can see it written after the closing bracket

EXAMPLE
[sc 2, sc-inc] 5 times

You crochet two single crochet stitches over the first 2 stitches (1 sc into the first stitch and 1 sc into the second stitch = sc 2).

Then you single crochet increase into the third stitch (crochet 2 single crochet stitches into the same stitch to increase).

Now you repeat the sequence of [2 sc and a single crochet increase] until you've worked the sequence 5 times in total.

> Just like crochet terms, insects have their own cipher language. While some use scent marks, sounds or light, bees prefer to dance their instructions.

°...°

Work the instructions between °and° all into the same stitch or same spot.

EXAMPLE
hdc 3, °hdc 1 + dc 1°

Make 3 half double crochet stitches over the first 3 stitches (1 hdc into each stitch).

Next, crochet a cluster of 1 half double crochet stitch **and** 1 double crochet stitch both into the next stitch.

EXAMPLE
sc 2, [hdc 3, °hdc 1 + dc 1°] 7 times

Start the round with 2 single crochet stitches (1 sc in the first and 1 sc into the second stitch).

Next, follow the sequence written in brackets that has to be repeated 7 times.

Make 3 half double crochet stitches over the next 3 stitches (1 hdc into each stitch).

Next, crochet 1 half double crochet stitch **and** 1 double crochet stitch both into the next stitch.

Repeat the sequence of 3 hdc and the cluster of 1 hdc and 1 dc, another 6 times, so you've worked it the required 7 times in total.

(...)

The number written in round brackets tells you the total number of stitches after you've finished a row or round.

EXAMPLE
[sc 2, sc-inc] 5 times. (20)

You've made 20 stitches at the end of this round.

STITCHES

CHAIN STITCH (CH)

Wrap the yarn around the hook (yo) and pull through the loop on the hook to create 1 chain stitch.

SLIP STITCH (SLST)

Insert hook into the stitch, yo and pull through the stitch and also the loop on the hook in one go.

SINGLE CROCHET (SC)

Insert the hook into the stitch, yo and pull through the stitch (2 loops are on your hook), yo again and pull through both loops on the hook in one go.

HALF DOUBLE CROCHET (HDC)

Yo, insert hook into the stitch, yo and pull the yarn through the stitch (3 loops are on your hook), yo and pull through all 3 loops on the hook in one go.

DOUBLE CROCHET (DC)

Yo, insert hook into the stitch, yo and pull the yarn through the stitch (3 loops are on your hook), yo and pull through the first 2 loops on the hook in one go (2 loops remain on the hook), yo again and draw through the remaining 2 loops.

TRIPLE CROCHET (TR)

Yo twice, insert hook into the stitch, yo and pull the yarn through the stitch (4 loops on hook), yo and pull through the first 2 loops on the hook (3 loops remain on hook), yo and pull through the first 2 loops again (2 loops remain on hook), yo and pull through the remaining 2 loops on the hook.

Work 4 unfinished double crochet stitches into one stitch (5 loops on hook).

Finish the bobble stitch by drawing the yarn through all 5 loops on the hook in one go.

BOBBLE STITCHES:

Bobble stitches are created with the wrong side of the fabric facing you (see photos 1 and 2), with the bobbles showing on the right side (see photo 3).

Ch 2.

Insert hook into front loop and bar.

Slip stitch, done.

BOBBLE STITCH (BL)

Wrap the yarn around the hook (yo), insert hook into the stitch, yo and pull the yarn through the stitch, yo and draw yarn through the first 2 loops on the hook (2 loops remain).

Yo, insert hook into same stitch, yo and pull the yarn through the stitch, yo and draw yarn through the first 2 loops on the hook (3 loops remain).

Yo, insert hook into same stitch, yo and pull the yarn through the stitch, yo and draw yarn through the first 2 loops on the hook (4 loops remain).

Yo, insert hook into same stitch, yo and pull the yarn through the stitch, yo and draw yarn through the first 2 loops on the hook (5 loops on hook).

Yo, pull the yarn through all 5 loops on hook in one go (see photos 1 and 2).

PICOT STITCH (CH2PICOT, CH1PICOT)

CH2PICOT

Ch 2, insert hook into the front loop and the upper bar of the post of the last dc (or tr). Crochet 1 slst in here (see photos 4–6.)

CH1PICOT

For a smaller version of this picot stitch work just one chain stitch before you slip stitch back into the loop and the upper part of the previous stitch.

Get to the point with picot stitch!

60

TUTORIALS

MAGIC LOOP

Make a loop from your yarn and pinch the join of the loop together with your thumb (this is the point where the yarn crosses) (see photo 1).

On the back of your hand, insert the hook into the loop and pull the yarn that is attached to the ball through the loop (see photo 2).

Crochet 1 chain stitch – see photo 3 – (this stitch doesn't count as st). This stitch fixes the loop and you can let go of the join of the loop.

Next, work the required stitches into the loop (see photo 4): insert hook into the loop (under the two strands of yarn that are twisted – the one that forms the ring and the one that is the tail). Wrap yarn around the hook (yo) and pull through the loop, yo again and pull through the 2 loops to finish your first single crochet stitch.

When all the required stitches of the first round are complete, pull the hanging yarn tail to close the central gap (see photo 5).

(For more, see tutorial video on www.lalylala.com.)

STARTING THE NEXT ROUND

Depending on what the pattern calls for, you will work in the round in one of two ways:

Method 1: Crochet directly into the first stitch of the round to start your second round (see photo 6).

Method 2: Close the round with a slst into the first stitch and start the second round with initial chain stitches (see photo 7).

1

2

3

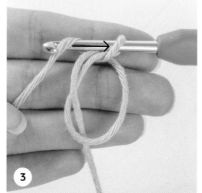

4

TALLER STITCHES:

If you make the magic loop with a round of taller stitches such as hdc or dc stitches, crochet the required number of chain stitches first (as indicated in the pattern), before you start to work your stitches into the loop.

5

6

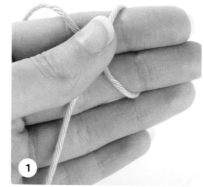

7

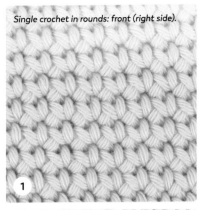
Single crochet in rounds: front (right side).

1

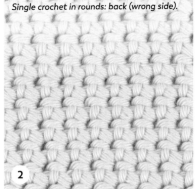
Single crochet in rounds: back (wrong side).

2

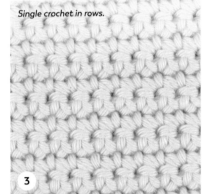
Single crochet in rows.

3

NOTE:

On the front side of single crochet worked in rounds, you can spot little 'V's on the surface, while the back is easy to identify from the horizontal lines of the back bumps on the stitches. Where single crochet is worked in rows, the front and back sides look alike with 'V's and back bumps on both sides.

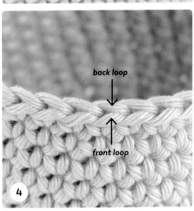
back loop

front loop

4

back bump (back bar)

5

RIGHT SIDE/WRONG SIDE OF THE CROCHETED FABRIC

For various reasons it can be important to distinguish what's the right side (front) or wrong side (back) of your crochet (e.g. if a pattern calls to work only into front or back loop of a stitch). In the photos 1–3 you can see the right and wrong side of single crochet stitches worked in rounds or in rows.

FRONT LOOPS/BACK LOOPS

FRONT LOOP

The front loop is the loop closest to you. If the crochet pattern says to work through front loop only (e.g. scflo), you will work your stitches just into this front loop (see photo 4).

BACK LOOP

The back loop is furthest away from you. If the crochet pattern says to work through back loop only (e.g. scblo), you will work into this back loop only (see photo 4).

BACK BUMPS

The back bump, or back bar, lies right behind the back loop of a stitch. Working into this spot leaves you with a visible line of stitches ('V's) on the surface of your fabric. You can use it also to create a well defined 90-degree nook (see photo 5).

FRONT/BACK OF A FOUNDATION CHAIN

On the front (right side) of your chain, the stitches are smooth and look like a series of interlocking 'V's (see photo 1).

On the back (wrong) side of your chain, the stitches are bumpy (see photo 2).

Working into the back bumps along a chain creates a neater finish.

SINGLE CROCHET DECREASE (SC2TOG)

INVISIBLE SINGLE CROCHET DECREASE FOR 3-DIMENSIONAL PIECES

Insert the hook into the front loop of the first stitch and then directly also into the front loop of the second stitch that you want to decrease. You now have both front loops and the loop of your last finished stitch on your hook (3 loops) (see photo 3).

Wrap the yarn around the hook (yo) and draw through both front loops on the hook in one go (see photos 3 and 4).

Yo again and draw through both loops on your hook to finish a single crochet stitch as usual (see photos 4 and 5).

STANDARD SINGLE CROCHET DECREASE

Insert the hook into the first stitch.

Wrap the yarn around the hook (yo) and pull a loop through the stitch (2 loops on hook).

Insert the hook into the second stitch.

Yo and pull through the stitch (3 loops on hook).

Yo again and pull through all 3 loops on your hook in one go.

Foundation chain: right side.

Foundation chain: wrong side.

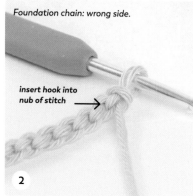

insert hook into nub of stitch →

1

2

3

4

Crochet with care – slow and steady wins the race!

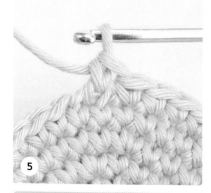

5

NOTE:

Use the invisible single crochet decrease for 3-dimensional pieces. (The invisible decrease also works for taller stitches, such as hdc or dc.)

On flat pieces, which also show the wrong side of the fabric, use the standard single crochet decrease.

STANDARD DECREASE WITH HDC STITCH (HDC2TOG)

Wrap the yarn around the hook (yo).

Insert the hook into the first stitch.

Yo and pull a loop through the stitch (3 loops on hook).

Insert the hook into the second stitch.

Yo and pull through the stitch (4 loops on hook).

Yo again and pull through all 4 loops on your hook in one go.

NOTE:

For hdc stitch worked over 3 stitches (**hdc3tog**), insert hook into third stitch and pull through the stitch (5 loops on hook); yo again and pull through all 5 loops on your hook in one go.

STANDARD DECREASE WITH DC STITCH (DC2TOG)

Wrap the yarn around the hook (yo), insert the hook into the first stitch.

Yo and pull a loop through the stitch (3 loops on hook).

Yo and pull through the first 2 loops on the hook (2 loops on hook).

Yo, insert the hook into the second stitch.

Yo and pull through the stitch (4 loops on hook).

Yo again and pull through the first 2 stitches on the hook (3 loops on hook).

Yo and draw through the remaining 3 loops on the hook in one go.

STANDARD DECREASE WITH TR STITCH (TR2TOG)

Wrap the yarn around the hook (yo) twice, insert the hook into the first stitch.

Yo and pull a loop through the stitch (4 loops on hook).

Yo and pull through the first 2 loops on the hook (3 loops on the hook).

Yo and pull through the first 2 loops on the hook again (2 loops on the hook).

Yo twice, insert the hook into the second stitch.

Yo and pull through the stitch (5 loops on the hook).

Yo and pull through the first 2 loops on the hook (4 loops on the hook).

Yo and pull through the first 2 loops on the hook again (3 loops on the hook).

Yo and draw through the remaining 3 loops on the hook in one go.

CHANGING TO A NEW YARN COLOUR

You will change to another colour by joining in the new colour during the final step of the last stitch in the old colour as follows: work the last stitch in the old colour until the last two loops of the stitch are on the hook, then using the new colour, wrap the yarn around the hook and pull through the 2 remaining old coloured loops on your hook (see photo 1). The next stitch you make will be the first stitch in the new colour.

JOIN YARN WITH A STANDING SC

Make a slip knot onto hook then insert hook into indicated stitch, wrap yarn around hook and pull loop through (see photo 2), wrap yarn around hook and pull through 2 loops to complete the single crochet (see photos 3 and 4).

JOIN YARN WITH A SLIP KNOT

Make a slip knot from your yarn (do not place on hook). Insert hook into indicated stitch. Place the slip knot onto hook (see photo 5) and pull the slip knot through the stitch (see photo 6). Take care to keep the knot on the back of the fabric. Work into the next stitch, or make the number of chains as indicated in the pattern (e.g. to start a new round).

You can also just insert hook into indicated stitch, wrap yarn around hook and pull it through the stitch if you prefer (without making a slip knot).

WEAVE IN ENDS AS YOU GO:

On 3-dimensional pieces, you can weave in the initial yarn tail of the new yarn and the remaining tail from the old yarn as you go by 'carrying' both threads.

To do this, lay both threads along the edge on top of the stitches to be worked and crochet over the strands for the next 4–5 stitches.

STANDING STITCH JOIN:

Joining your yarn with a standing stitch means that an initiating chain stitch is not required. The standing stitch look identical to the standard crochet stitch and counts as 1 stitch.

You can join yarn with taller standing stitches: e.g. for standing dc, pinch the knot of the slip knot so it can't move, then yo, insert hook into st and work a standard dc as usual.

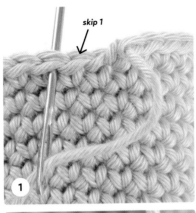

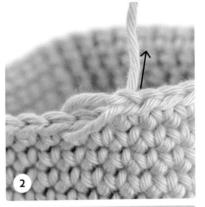

skip 1

NOTE:

When you fasten off invisibly, you get a smooth finish with even edge sts. For an extra nice finish, work an additional slst before you fasten off.

On pieces made with taller stitches, you may need to bring down the working loop with smaller sts: e.g. if last st is dc, crochet 1–2 hdc, 1–2 sc, 1 slst additionally to bring working loop as close to the edge as possible.

FASTEN OFF

Break the yarn and pull the yarn tail through the last loop on your hook completely. Pull on the tail to tighten down the chain stitch.

FASTEN OFF INVISIBLY

Cut yarn, pull the yarn tail through the last stitch completely and thread yarn tail onto yarn/tapestry needle. Skip one stitch then insert needle into the next stitch in the same way as you would your crochet hook (see photo 1). Next, insert needle back into the same stitch that the yarn tail is coming from but into the back loop only. Pull gently (see photo 2) – this creates a false stitch (or a closing stitch) that mimics the skipped stitch (see photo 3). Weave tail into wrong side before trimming.

CLOSING REMAINING STITCHES (THROUGH THE FRONT LOOPS)

Cut yarn, pull the yarn tail through the last stitch completely and thread yarn tail onto yarn/tapestry needle.

Insert needle through the front loops only of each remaining stitch from outside to inside (see photo 4).

Pull gently to close the gap (see photos 5 and 6).

Stitch through the crochet piece in any direction and come out through a stitch on the other side; tie a knot as close on the surface as you can, cut the tail above the knot and pull knot and the tiny yarn end just above the knot back inside the fabric (see photo 7).

CLOSING REMAINING STITCHES (THROUGH THE BACK LOOPS)

Cut yarn and pull the end through the last stitch completely. Thread yarn tail onto yarn/tapestry needle.

Insert needle through the back loops only of each remaining stitch from inside to outside (see photo 1).

Pull gently to close the gap (see photo 2).

Stitch through the crochet piece in any direction and come out through a stitch on the other side; tie a knot as close on the surface as you can, cut the tail above the knot and pull knot and the tiny yarn end just above the knot back inside the fabric (see photo 3).

1

2

3

NOTE:

On pieces made worked into the back loops only, this finishing technique gives you a continuous spiral of remaining front loops until the very end. This is extra neat if you want to crochet or embroider into the front loops in a future step.

WEAVING IN ENDS ON BACK SIDE OF THE FABRIC

Thread a needle with the remaining yarn tail and use the back bumps on the back side of the fabric to weave in the ends. Pull through 5 or 6 bars upwards, head over to the next back bar on the left or right and pull the yarn through 5–6 bumps downwards. Head to the next back bump and pull through 5–6 bumps upwards again. You can also weave in in horizontal direction by using one of the legs of the stitches to insert the needle.

On fabric made from taller stitches, you sew into the bars on the back (wrong side) of the posts of the stitches.

WEAVING IN/ FASTENING OFF ENDS INSIDE A 3-DIMENSIONAL PIECE

Thread a needle with the remaining yarn tail. Stitch the needle all the way through the stuffed crochet piece and come out through a stitch on the other side. Take care not to stitch through the yarn but through the free space between stitches. Pull the yarn tail gently, keeping it tight, and make a knot as close on the surface as you can. Cut off the tail above the knot and use a needle or hook to pull the knot through the stitch back inside the crochet piece, so it can't be seen from the outside.

1

2

FITTING TOY SAFETY EYES

> **SAFETY NOTE:**
> Do not use toy safety eyes if giving to a child under 3 years of age. Instead, use black or grey yarn to embroider eyes.

Safety eyes consist of two pieces – the eye, with a smooth or a threaded rod, and the washer (plastic or metal).

Insert the eyes from the right side in the correct position, following the pattern (see photo 1). Make sure you are happy with the placement before proceeding because once the washer is fixed to the rod of the eye, it cannot be removed.

Carefully turn the head inside out and fix the washer onto the rod, pressing it down firmly to lock it in place (see photo 2).

ASSEMBLING BUTTERFLY WINGS

Referring to Sewing Technique 1, sew together both pairs of large and small wings for the left and the right side along the pink dotted lines (see photo 3). Then sew each pair of wings vertically, along the marked solid blue line, left and right from the seam that was made to close the belt to a ring. Add a couple of stitches on the left and right to make the wings more stable so that they are secured on the belt (see blue dotted marks).

When the wings are sewn securely onto the belt (see photo 4), sew the wing cover in the middle of the back of the wing cluster with the tip point upwards (see photo 5). Do not sew through the top of the stitches of the wing cover, instead sew around the posts of the stitches.

3

4

5

SEWING TECHNIQUES

TECHNIQUE 1: SEWING EDGES OF FLAT PARTS TOGETHER (E.G. FOR WING CLUSTERS)

1. Pin the pieces together according to the pattern instructions.

2. Use matching coloured yarn threaded onto a yarn/tapestry needle.

3. Insert needle up through a stitch on piece A and directly through the corresponding space before one stitch on piece B (photo 1). Then insert needle down through the next space along on piece B (so you are working around the post of a stitch) (see photo 2).

4. Take needle to piece A and insert into the same space the yarn comes from and out through the next space along (you are working around the post of the stitch). Pull yarn gently to tighten (see photo 3).

5. Repeat Steps 3 and 4 and pull yarn tight after every few stitches. Continue until the seam is complete.

6. Tie off yarn ends and weave ends.

TECHNIQUE 2: SEWING ONTO THE SURFACE OF A 3-DIMENSIONAL PIECE (E.G. FOR SNAIL TENTACLES)

1. Pin the pieces together according to the pattern instructions.

2. Use the remaining yarn tail from the piece (B) that you want to sew onto a base piece (A). Thread yarn tail onto a yarn/tapestry needle. Insert needle down into first stitch on base piece A and come up through the next stitch along (so you are working around the post of a stitch).

3. Go up through the first stitch on piece B, inserting the needle under both loops of the stitch towards you, from the inside of the piece towards outside (see photo 4) (if there's just one loop left, as for the snail's shell, you insert the needle just into that single loop). Pull yarn through.

4. Go back to piece A and insert the needle into the same stitch as where the yarn comes from and come up through the next stitch along (so you are working around the post of the next stitch) (see photo 5). Insert the needle into the next stitch on piece B, as you did in Step 3 and pull the yarn through.

5. Repeat Step 4 and pull yarn tight after every few stitches. Continue until the seam is almost complete and, if necessary, add more toy filling before stitching the remaining seam closed.

6. Tie off yarn ends and weave ends into one piece (for the snail, into the tentacle).

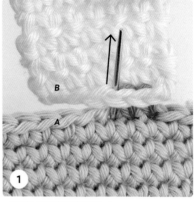

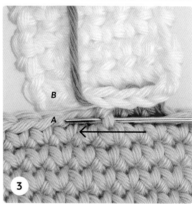

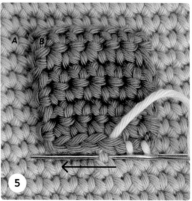

PATTERNS

THE MAGICAL METAMORPHOSIS
OF A BALL OF YARN

On the following pages, you'll not only find detailed descriptions for the crochet anatomy of our tiny insect friends, but also many useful tips to help you to create them as perfectly as nature does.

While all the patterns are suitable for beginners and crochet pros alike, those less experienced might want to start with one of the smallest creatures, the aphid, to familiarise themselves with crochet terms and pattern structure.

The aphid is easy as pie and fast to make and before you know it, you'll have created a little colony of aphids. Then you can move on to the caterpillar, and make her a plain egg (unbobbled) and her first set of butterfly wings, starting with the easy brimstone butterfly wing suit. Once you to have got the knack of it, the more complex instructions are a snap.

If you are an experienced crocheter, take your crochet hook and pick any pattern you choose!

EGG

FOR MAGGOT, BEETLE AND SNAIL

MATERIALS

HOOK SIZE: US C/2 (2.5mm or 2.25mm)

YARN: Scheepjes Catona 4ply (sport), 100% cotton, 25g/62m

· 1 ball of Shade 100 Lemon Chiffon (light yellow)

OTHER RECOMMENDED COLOUR SHADES

· 263 Petal Peach (pale peach)
· 101 Candle Light (pale lemon)
· 130 Old Lace (off-white)
· 509 Baby Blue (pale blue)
· 505 Linen (cream)

NOTE:

Always work the first stitch into the base of the beginning chain.

Always close the round with a slst into the top of the first hdc (not into the beginning chain). This creates a less visible join when working in the round.

PATTERN

Using chosen colour, make a magic loop (see Tutorials).

Round 1: ch 2 (not counted as a stitch on any round), hdc 8 into magic loop, slst to top of first hdc, turn. (8 sts)

Round 2: ch 2, hdc-inc in every st, slst to top of first hdc, turn. (16 sts)

Round 3: ch 2, [hdc 1, hdc-inc] 8 times, slst to top of first hdc, turn. (24 sts)

Round 4: ch 2, hdc 1, hdc-inc, [hdc 2, hdc-inc] 7 times, hdc 1, slst to top of first hdc, turn. (32 sts)

Round 5: ch 2, [hdc 3, hdc-inc] 8 times, slst to top of first hdc, turn. (40 sts)

Round 6: ch 2, hdc 40, slst to top of first hdc, turn.

Round 7: ch 2, hdc 40.

Break yarn and fasten off the round invisibly (see Tutorials) into the top of the first hdc (we will call this fake stitch a 'closing stitch').

Starting from the closing stitch, count 17 stitches along then insert the hook into the 17th stitch, from the inside towards the outside (see photo 1) and join yarn with a slip knot (see Tutorials).

Continue in rows.

Row 8: ch 2, [hdc2tog] twice, hdc 24, [hdc2tog] twice, turn, leaving remaining stitches unworked. (28 sts)

Row 9: ch2, [hdc2tog] twice, hdc 20, [hdc2tog] twice, turn. (24 sts)

Rows 10–12: ch2, hdc 24, turn (3 rows).

Row 13: ch2, hdc-inc, hdc 22, hdc-inc, turn. (26 sts)

Row 14: ch2, °hdc 3°, hdc 24, °hdc 3°, ch10. (30 hdc, 10 ch)

Take care not to twist the chain and close the round with a slst into the top of the first hdc on the opposite side of the opening (see photo 2), place a stitch marker into the slst, break yarn and fasten off invisibly.

Count 16 stitches forwards, starting in the marked slst. Insert the hook into the 16th stitch, from outside towards inside (see photo 3) and join the yarn with a slip knot (see Tutorials).

Continue in rounds.

Round 15: ch 2, hdc 1 in same st at base of ch 2, hdc 14, hdc 1 into the back loop of the slst, hdc 10 into the back loops along the chain, hdc 14, slst to top of first hdc, turn. (40 sts)

Rounds 16–18: ch 2, hdc 40, slst to top of first hdc, turn (3 rounds).

Round 19: ch 2, hdc 4, hdc2tog, [hdc 8, hdc2tog] 3 times, hdc 4, slst to top of first hdc, turn. (36 sts)

Round 20: ch 2, hdc 36, slst to top of first hdc, turn.

Round 21: ch 2, [hdc 7, hdc2tog] 4 times, slst to top of first hdc, turn. (32 sts)

Round 22: ch 2, hdc 32, slst to top of first hdc, turn.

Round 23: ch 2, [hdc 2, hdc2tog] 8 times, slst to top of first hdc, turn. (24 sts)

Round 24: ch 2, [hdc 1, hdc2tog] 8 times, slst to top of first hdc, turn. (16 sts)

Round 25: ch 2, [hdc2tog] 8 times. (8 sts)

Break the yarn and close remaining 8 stitches through the front loops (see Tutorials).

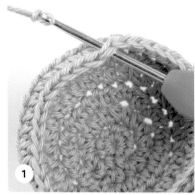

FINISHING

Crochet a tidy border of single crochet stitches around the opening and weave in all ends on the inside of the egg.

EGG

FOR BUTTERFLY AND MOTH

MATERIALS

HOOK SIZE: US C/2 (2.5mm or 2.25mm)

YARN: Scheepjes Catona 4ply (sport), 100% cotton, 25g/62m

· 1 ball of Shade 130 Old Lace (off-white)

OTHER RECOMMENDED COLOUR SHADES

· 263 Petal Peach (pale peach)

· 100 Lemon Chiffon (light yellow)

· 101 Candle Light (pale lemon)

· 509 Baby Blue (pale blue)

· 505 Linen (cream)

NOTE:

Always work the first stitch into the base of the beginning chain.

Always close the round with a slst into the top of the first hdc (not into the beginning chain). This creates a less visible join when working in the round.

Refer to Tutorials for more advice on working bobble sitch (bl).

PATTERN

Using chosen colour, make a magic loop (see Tutorials).

Round 1: ch 2 (not counted as a stitch on any round), hdc 8 into magic loop, slst to top of first hdc, turn. (8 sts)

Round 2: ch 2, [°bl 1 + hdc 1°] 8 times, slst to top of first bl, turn. (16 sts)

Round 3: ch 2, [hdc 1, hdc-inc] 8 times, slst to top of first hdc, turn. (24 sts)

Round 4: ch 2, hdc 1, °bl 1 + hdc 1°, [hdc 2, °bl 1 + hdc 1°] 7 times, hdc 1, slst to top of first hdc, turn. (32 sts)

Round 5: ch 2, [hdc 3, hdc-inc] 8 times, slst to top of first hdc, turn. (40 sts)

Round 6: ch 2, hdc 2, bl 1, [hdc 4, bl 1] 7 times, hdc 2, slst to top of first hdc, turn.

Round 7: ch 2, hdc 40.

Break the yarn and fasten off invisibly (see Tutorials) into the top of the **second** hdc (we will call this fake stitch a 'closing stitch'). Weave in the end on the inside.

Starting in the closing stitch, count 16 stitches along then insert the hook into the 16th stitch, from inside, towards outside and join yarn with a slip knot (see Tutorials).

Continue in rows.

Row 8: ch 2, skip 1, bl 1, [hdc 4, bl 1] 5 times, hdc2tog, turn, leaving remaining sts unworked. (27 sts)

Row 9: ch 2, hdc3tog, hdc 21, hdc3tog, turn. (23 sts)

Row 10: ch 2, hdc 3, bl 1, [hdc 4, bl 1] 3 times, hdc 2, hdc2tog, turn. (22 sts)

Row 11: ch 2, hdc 22, turn.

Row 12: ch 2, hdc 3, bl 1, [hdc 4, bl 1] 3 times, hdc 3, turn.

Row 13: ch 2, hdc-inc, hdc 20, hdc-inc, turn. (24 sts)

Row 14: ch 2, °hdc 1 + bl 1°, hdc-inc, hdc 2, bl 1, [hdc 4, bl 1] 3 times, hdc 2, hdc-inc, °bl 1 + hdc 1°, ch 12. (28 hdc + 12 ch)

Take care not to twist the chain and close the round with a slst into the top of the first hdc on other side of opening. Place marker into slst, break yarn and fasten off invisibly (see photo 1).

Find the stitch in the very middle between the two bobbles on the centre back. Insert the hook from outside towards inside through this stitch (see photo 2) and join yarn with a slip knot (see Tutorials).

Continue in rounds.

Round 15: ch 2, hdc 1 in same st at base of ch 2, hdc 13, hdc 1 into the back loop of the slst (remove marker from slst), hdc 12 into the back loops along the chain, hdc 13, slst to top of first hdc, turn. (40 sts)

Round 16: ch 2, hdc 2, bl 1, [hdc 4, bl 1] 7 times, hdc 2, slst to top of first hdc, turn.

Round 17: ch 2, hdc 40, slst to top of first hdc, turn.

Round 18: ch 2, hdc 2, bl 1, [hdc 4, bl 1] 7 times, hdc 2, slst to top of first hdc, turn.

Round 19: ch 2, hdc 4, hdc2tog, [hdc 8, hdc2tog] 3 times, hdc 4, slst to top of first hdc, turn. (36 sts)

Round 20: ch 2, hdc 2, bl 1, [hdc 3, bl 1, hdc 4, bl 1] 3 times, hdc 3, bl 1, hdc 2, slst to top of first hdc, turn.

Round 21: ch 2, [hdc 7, hdc2tog] 4 times, slst to top of first hdc, turn. (32 sts)

Round 22: ch 2, hdc 1, bl 1, [hdc 3, bl 1] 7 times, hdc 2, slst to top of first hdc, turn.

Round 23: ch 2, hdc 1, hdc2tog, [hdc 2, hdc2tog] 7 times, hdc 1, slst to top of first hdc, turn. (24 sts)

Round 24: ch 2, skip 1st stitch, [bl 1, hdc2tog] 7 times, bl 1, hdc 1, slst to top of first bl, turn. (16 sts)

Round 25: ch 2, [hdc2tog] 8 times. (8 sts)

Break the yarn and close the remaining 8 stitches through the front loops (see Tutorials).

FINISHING

Crochet a tidy border of half double crochet stitches around the opening and weave in all ends inside the egg.

BASIC SHAPES

Some of the parts of many of the creatures are made in the same way, such as the head and the hat for example, and the pattern instructions for all the repeat elements are given in this section.

For the yarn colours to use for the basic shapes of your chosen bug, see the individual patterns.

HEAD

TOP-DOWN (BUTTERFLIES, MOTH, FLY, BEETLES)

See individual butterfly/moth/fly/beetle pattern for yarn colour to use.

Using **recommended colour**, make a magic loop (see Tutorials).

Round 1: sc 7 into magic loop. (7 sts)

Round 2: sc-inc in every st. (14 sts)

Round 3: [sc 1, sc-inc] 7 times. (21 sts)

Round 4: sc 1, sc-inc, [sc 2, sc-inc] 6 times, sc 1. (28 sts)

Round 5: [sc 3, sc-inc] 7 times. (35 sts)

Round 6: sc 35.

Round 7: sc 2, sc-inc, [sc 4, sc-inc] 6 times, sc 2. (42 sts)

Rounds 8–13: sc 42 (6 rounds).

Place the eyes between Rounds 12 and 13 with a distance of 9 stitches between each eye (see Tutorials).

Round 14: sc 2, sc2tog, [sc 4, sc2tog] 6 times, sc 2. (35 sts)

Round 15: [sc2tog, sc 3] 7 times. (28 sts)

Round 16: sc 1, sc2tog, [sc 2, sc2tog] 6 times, sc 1. (21 sts)

For beetles, stuff the head and change yarn to the colour of the body in the last step of the last sc in Round 16 (see Tutorials).

For butterflies, moth and fly, work an additional round of decreases:

Round 17: [sc2tog, sc 1] 7 times. (14 sts)

Stuff the head and change yarn to the colour of the body in the last step of the last sc in Round 17 (see Tutorials).

BOTTOM-UP (SNAIL)

Change to **off-white** in the last step of the last stitch:

Round 1: [scflo 1, scflo-inc] 7 times. (21 sts)

Round 2: sc 1, sc-inc, [sc 2, sc-inc] 6 times, sc 1. (28 sts)

Round 3: [sc 3, sc-inc] 7 times. (35 sts)

Round 4: sc 2, sc-inc, [sc 4, sc-inc] 6 times, sc 2. (42 sts)

Rounds 5–10: sc 42 (6 rounds).

Place the eyes between Rounds 5 and 6 with a distance of 9 stitches between each eye (see Tutorials).

Round 11: sc 2, sc2tog, [sc 4, sc2tog] 6 times, sc 2. (35 sts)

Round 12: sc 35.

Round 13: [sc2tog, sc 3] 7 times. (28 sts)

Round 14: sc 1, sc2tog, [sc 2, sc2tog] 6 times, sc 1. (21 sts)

Stuff the head.

Round 15: [sc2tog, sc 1] 7 times. (14 sts)

Round 16: [sc2tog] 7 times. (7 sts)

Break the yarn and stuff the head a little more, then close the remaining stitches through the front loops (see Tutorials) and weave in the ends.

FINISHING

Use some powder pink yarn to embroider cheeks underneath your bug's eyes. Alternatively, use light pink fabric marker or rouge/blusher.

HAT

See the individual bug pattern for the colour to use.

Using **recommended colour**, make a magic loop (see Tutorials).

Round 1: sc 7 into magic loop. (7 sts)

Round 2: sc-inc in every st. (14 sts)

Round 3: [sc 1, sc-inc] 7 times. (21 sts)

Round 4: sc 1, sc-inc, [sc 2, sc-inc] 6 times, sc 1. (28 sts)

Round 5: [sc 3, sc-inc] 7 times. (35 sts)

Round 6: sc 35.

Round 7: sc 2, sc-inc, [sc 4, sc-inc] 6 times, sc 2. (42 sts)

Rounds 8–14: sc 42 (7 rounds).

> **NOTE:**
> After Round 14, pull the hat onto the head and decide whether it fits properly, pulling it down to sit on the base of the neck (remembering that there's a final round to work). If it seems a little too short, crochet one more straight round. If it fits, you can continue with Round 15.

STANDARD PLAIN EDGE

Round 15: sc 2, sc2tog, [sc 4, sc2tog] 6 times, sc 2. (35 sts)

POINTY BEETLE EDGE

Round 15: [sc 3, sc2tog] 3 times, sc 3, hdc 1, dc 1, ch1picot (see Stitches), dc 1, hdc 1, [sc 3, sc2tog] 4 times. (35 sts)

Slst 1 into the next stitch, break the yarn and fasten off invisibly (see Tutorials).

> I don't mean to be a pain in the neck, but do put my hat on properly, please.

ANTENNAE (MAKE 2)

TYPE A (BUTTERFLIES, BEETLES AND FLY)

Make a foundation chain of 4 ch, starting in the 2nd bump on the back of the chain: sc 1, slst 2 into the back bumps along the chain (see Tutorials).

Break the yarn and fasten off, leaving a long tail for sewing the antenna onto the hat.

TYPE B (MOTH)

Make a foundation chain of 7 ch, starting in the 2nd bump on the back of the chain: slst 6 into the back bumps along the chain.

Break the yarn and fasten off, leaving a long tail for sewing the antenna onto the hat.

MOTH ANTENNAE FRINGES

Cut three pieces of yarn about 10cm (4in) long. Take the first antenna wrong side facing you and insert the hook into the front loop of the second slst from top. Grab the piece of yarn at its middle and pull a loop halfway through. Wrap the ends around the hook, pull through the loop on the hook and pull tight. Tie two more strands onto the antenna in the same way. Finally cut all six strands to a height of 1cm (⅜in).

Repeat for the second antenna, but this time with the right side of the antenna facing you.

ATTACHING THE ANTENNAE TO THE HAT

Sew the antennae onto the hat – right above the 3rd round counting upwards from the rim, with a distance of 2 stitches between the antennae.

I'm so sensitive – I blame it on my antennae!

BELT

The belt – a crochet rectangle finished into a ring – is what the bug's wings will be attached to, to create a wing suit that can be pulled on and off, to turn a caterpillar into a butterfly or a moth.

See individual patterns for colour to use.

TYPE A (BUTTERFLIES AND MOTH)

Using **recommended colour**, ch 12.

Row 1: starting in 2nd ch from hook, slstblo 11, turn. (11 sts)

Rows 2–35: ch 1, starting in 2nd stitch from hook (skip turning ch), slstblo 11, turn (34 rows).

Do not fasten off.

FINISHING

Turn the rectangle into a ring by holding the first and last rows next to each other. Crochet together the remaining loops of the foundation chain on the bottom of the first row with the corresponding back loops of the stitches on the last row (see photo 1). Slst the ends together stitch by stitch. Break yarn and fasten off. Weave in the ends on the inside of the belt.

For the moth belt, brush the outside of the fabric with a soft wire brush until it is fuzzy.

Sew the wing pairs onto the belt, left and right of the seam (see Tutorials).

TYPE B (FLY)

Row 1: ch 12, starting in 2nd ch from hook, scblo 11, turn. (11 sts)

Rows 2: ch 1, starting in 2nd stitch from hook (skip turning chain), scblo 8, slst 3, turn.

Row 3: ch 1, scblo 11, turn.

Repeat Row 2 and Row 3 alternately 9 times more, then repeat Row 2 one more time (23 rows worked).

FINISHING

Follow instructions as given for Type A (butterflies and moth) belt, but do not break the yarn when you've closed the rectangle into a ring and do not sew the wings onto the belt yet.

To crochet on, go back to the fly pattern (see Fly).

WING COVER

The wing cover (see photo 2) hides the point where the wings are joined to the belt on the back of the wing suit.

See individual patterns for colour to use.

Using **recommended colour**, ch 5.

Round 1: starting in 2nd ch from hook, sc 1, hdc 1, dc 1, °dc 7° into the last ch, rotate 180 degrees and crochet along the opposite side of the foundation chain: dc 1, hdc 1, sc 1. (13 sts)

Break the yarn with a very long tail and fasten off invisibly into the first stitch (see Tutorials).

FINISHING

After sewing the wings onto the belt, cover the point where the wings join with the wing cover and sew in place (see Tutorials) (photo 3).

CATERPILLARS

All three caterpillar types follow the same basic body shape with pattern variations to make a plain one (P), one with narrow stripes (S1), or one with wide stripes (S2). Follow the colour indicators in front of each round for the yarn colours to use for your chosen caterpillar.

Hey, you are holding the book upside down!

MATERIALS

HOOK SIZE: US C/2 (2.25mm or 2.5mm)

YARN: Scheepjes Catona 4ply (sport), 100% cotton, 25g/62m

For Plain Caterpillar (P) – 1 ball of each shade
- Yarn A 130 Old Lace (off white)
- Yarn B 402 Silver Green (pale sage)

For Narrow Striped Caterpillar (S1) – 1 ball of each shade
- Yarn A 130 Old Lace (off white)
- Yarn C 383 Ginger Gold (golden brown)
- Yarn D 501 Anthracite (dark grey)
- Yarn E 101 Candle Light (pale yellow)

For Wide Striped Caterpillar (S2) – 1 ball of each shade
- Yarn A 130 Old Lace (off white)
- Yarn C 383 Ginger Gold (golden brown)
- Yarn D 501 Anthracite (dark grey)
- Yarn F 110 Jet Black (black)

YOU ALSO NEED:
- Toy filling
- 5mm black toy safety eyes

PATTERN

HEAD

Using **off white**, follow the top-down head pattern (see Basic Shapes: Head Pattern) to the end of Round 17, changing to yarn B (for caterpillar type P), yarn D (for caterpillar type S1) and yarn F (for caterpillar type S2) in the last step of the last stitch of the round.

BODY

Note: The letters represent the colour for each round when working each of the caterpillars as listed in the following order: P, S1, S2.

B D F **Round 18:** slst 14. (14 sts)

B D F **Round 19:** [scblo 1, scblo-inc] 7 times. (21 sts)

B D F **Round 20:** sc 1, sc-inc, [sc 2, sc-inc] 6 times, sc 1. (28 sts)

B E D **Round 21:** sc 28.

B D D **Round 22:** sc 28.

B E F **Round 23:** sc 28.

B D F **Round 24:** sc 28.

B E D **Round 25:** sc 1, sc2tog, [sc 2, sc2tog] 6 times, sc 1. (21 sts)

B D D **Round 26:** [sc2tog, sc 1] 7 times. (14 sts)

B D F **Round 27:** slst 14.

B D F **Round 28:** [scflo 1, scflo-inc] 7 times. (21 sts)

B E F **Round 29:** sc 1, sc-inc, [sc 2, sc-inc] 6 times, sc 1. (28 sts)

Stuff the upper part of the body now.

B D D **Round 30:** sc 28.

B E D **Round 31:** sc 28.

B D F **Round 32:** sc 28.

B E F **Round 33:** sc 1, sc2tog, [sc 2, sc2tog] 6 times, sc 1. (21 sts)

B D F **Round 34:** [sc2tog, sc 1] 7 times. (14 sts)

B D D **Round 35:** slst 14.

B D D **Round 36:** [scflo 1, scflo-inc] 7 times. (21 sts)

B E D **Round 37:** sc 21.

Stuff the middle part of the body.

B D F **Round 38:** [sc2tog, sc 1] 7 times. (14 sts)

B D F **Round 39:** [sc2tog] 7 times. (7 sts)

Stuff the lower part of the body, then break the yarn.

Close the remaining 7 stitches through the front loops (see Tutorials) and weave in all ends.

HAT

Using yarn B (for caterpillar type P), yarn C (for caterpillar type S1) and yarn F (for caterpillar type and S2), follow the hat pattern with standard plain edge (see Basic Shapes: Hat Pattern).

COCOON

FOR BUTTERFLY AND MOTH

MATERIALS

HOOK SIZE: US C/2 (2.5mm or 2.25mm)

YARN: Scheepjes Catona 4ply (sport), 100% cotton, 25g/62m – 1 ball of each shade
- 205 Kiwi (lime green)
- 392 Lime Juice (light green)

PATTERN

Using **lime green**, ch 14.

Start in 2nd ch from hook:

Round 1: slst 3, sc 3, hdc 3, dc 3, dc 10 in last stitch, rotate and work along the opposite side of the foundation chain: dc 3, hdc 3, sc 3, slst 3, changing to **light green** on the last slst, ch 50. (84 sts)

Round 2: take care not to twist the chain and slst 1 into the back loop of the first slst on the tip of the drop shape; place marker into this stitch, slstblo 33, crochet into the back bumps on the back side of the chain (see Tutorials): sc 50. (84 sts)

Next, crochet the following stitches around the drop shape: hdcblo 1 into the back loop of the marked slst (remove marker), dcblo 32, hdcblo 1.

Mark the first stitch of Round 3 as the new beginning of all the following rounds.

From now on, crochet through back loops only (blo).

Round 3: dcblo 1 (pm here), dcblo 4, dc2tog-blo, [dcblo 5, dc2tog-blo] 11 times. (72 sts)

Round 4: dcblo 2, dc2tog-blo, [dcblo 4, dc2tog-blo] 11 times, dcblo 2. (60 sts)

Round 5: [dc2tog-blo, dcblo 3] 12 times. (48 sts)

Round 6: dcblo 1, dc2tog-blo, [dcblo 2, dc2tog-blo] 11 times, dcblo 1. (36 sts)

Round 7: [dc2tog-blo, dcblo 1] 12 times. (24 sts)

Round 8: [dc2tog-blo] 12 times. (12 sts)

Round 9: hdc-blo 1, sc-blo 1, leaving remaining stitches unworked.

Break yarn and close the remaining 12 stitches through the back loops (see Tutorials).

Cocoons are masters of mimicry. Some look like leaves, others have a mirror surface to reflect their environs.

HOOD

Mark the 26th stitch (number 1) and the 38th stitch (number 2) on the cocoon's margin, starting from the first light green stitch on the right side of the opening.

Join **light green** with a standing sc stitch (see Tutorials) into the marked stitch number 1 (cocoon's back side is facing you) (counts as first st).

Round 1: hdc 9, sc 1, slst 1, ch 26, slst 1 into marked stitch number 2, sc 1, hdc 10. (50 sts)

Round 2: slstblo 1, scblo 1, hdcblo 1, dcblo 9, now working into the back bumps of the chain: dc 12, dc2tog over the next stitch and the 3rd stitch (you skip one ch bump in between), dc 11 into the back bumps, dcblo 12. (48 sts)

Round 3: [dc2tog-blo, dcblo 2] 12 times. (36 sts)

Round 4: [dc2tog-blo, dcblo 1] 12 times. (24 sts)

Round 5: [dc2tog-blo] 12 times. (12 sts)

Round 6: [hdcblo 1, hdc2tog-blo] 4 times. (8 sts)

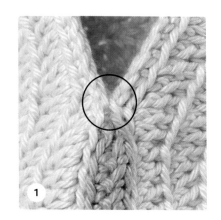

Sc 1 into the next stitch, break yarn and close the remaining 8 stitches through the back loops (see Tutorials).

Use the remaining yarn tail from the beginning to sew together the two light green stitches right above the tip of the drop shape on the front (see photo 1), then weave in the ends on the inside of the cocoon.

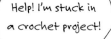

Help! I'm stuck in a crochet project!

BRIMSTONE BUTTERFLY (Gonepteryx rhamni)

MATERIALS

HOOK SIZE: US C/2 (2.25mm or 2.5mm)

YARN: Scheepjes Catona 4ply (sport), 100% cotton, 25g/62m – 1 ball of each shade

- 130 Old Lace (off-white)
- 100 Lemon Chiffon (light yellow)
- 280 Lemon (bright yellow)
- 101 Candle Light (pale yellow)
- 501 Anthracite (dark grey)
- 383 Ginger Gold (golden brown)

YOU ALSO NEED:

- Toy filling
- 5mm black toy safety eyes

PATTERN

HEAD

Using **off-white**, follow the top-down head pattern (see Basic Shapes: Head).

BODY

Using **dark grey** and **pale yellow**, follow the pattern for the narrow striped caterpillar body, type S1 (see Caterpillar: Body).

HAT

Using **golden brown**, follow the hat pattern with standard plain edge (see Basic Shapes: Hat).

ANTENNAE

Using **dark grey**, follow type A antennae pattern (see Basic Shapes: Antennae).

BELT

Using **dark grey**, follow type A belt pattern (see Basic Shapes: Belt).

WING COVER

Using **golden brown**, follow the wing cover pattern (see Basic Shapes: Wing Cover).

LARGE WINGS

RIGHT AND LEFT WING (MAKE 4)

Using **light yellow**, ch 6.

Start in 2nd ch from hook:

Round 1: sc 2, hdc 2, °dc 7°, rotate and continue into remaining loops on the opposite side of chain, hdc 2, sc 2, ch 2. (15 sts + ch-2sp)

Round 2: sc 4, hdc 1, hdc-inc, [dc-inc] 3 times, hdc-inc, hdc 1, sc 4, °sc 1 + ch 2 + sc 1° in ch-2sp (22 sts + ch-2sp)

Round 3: sc 6, hdc 1, hdc-inc, [dc-inc] 4 times, hdc-inc, hdc 1, sc 7, °sc 1 + ch 2 + sc 1° in ch-2sp, sc 1. (30 sts + ch-2sp)

Round 4: sc 8, hdc 1, hdc-inc, [dc 1, dc-inc] 3 times, dc 1, hdc-inc, hdc 1, sc 9, °sc 1 + ch 2 + sc 1° into ch-2sp, slst 1, leaving last stitch unworked. (36 sts + ch-2sp)

Break the yarn and close the round invisibly (see Tutorials). Make another 3 pieces in the same way.

ASSEMBLING 2 PIECES TO MAKE 1 WING

Hold 2 of the pieces together so they lay flat on top of each other, right sides outside. Insert the hook through the corresponding stitches or spaces of both layers to crochet them together in the next round.

The tip of the drop shape points to the right. Join **bright yellow** yarn with a standing sc (see Tutorials) into the ch-2sp on the tip (counts as first st).

RIGHT WING

Round 5: sc 2 into same ch-2sp as join, rotate 90 degrees clockwise, sc 13, sc-inc, hdc-inc, dc-inc, °dc 1 + tr 1°, tr 1, °tr 1 + dc 1°, dc-inc, hdc-inc, hdc 2, °hdc 1 + sc 1°, sc 13. (48 sts)

Break the yarn and fasten off invisibly into the stitch after the standing sc from the beginning.

LEFT WING

Round 5: sc 2 into same ch-2sp as join, rotate 90 degrees clockwise, sc 13, °sc 1 + hdc 1°, hdc 2, hdc-inc, dc-inc, °dc 1 + tr 1°, tr 1, °tr 1 + dc 1°, dc-inc, hdc-inc, sc-inc, sc 13. (48 sts)

Fasten off as for right wing.

SMALL WINGS

RIGHT AND LEFT WING (MAKE 4)

Using **light yellow**, ch 6.

Start in 2nd ch from hook:

Round 1: sc 2, hdc 2, °dc 7°, rotate and continue into remaining loops on the opposite side of chain: hdc 2, sc 2, ch 2. (15 sts + ch-2sp)

Round 2: sc 4, hdc 1, hdc-inc, [dc-inc] 3 times, hdc-inc, hdc 1, sc 4, °sc 1 + ch 2 + sc 1° in ch-2sp (22 sts + ch-2sp)

Break the yarn and close the round invisibly into the 2nd stitch of the round (see Tutorials). Make another 3 pieces in the same way.

A popular theory says that the word 'butterfly', as in 'a butter-coloured fly', originated to describe the Brimstone.

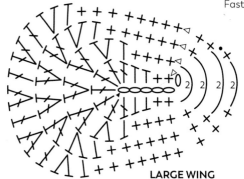

LARGE WING

SMALL WING

ASSEMBLING 2 PIECES TO MAKE 1 WING

Hold 2 of the pieces together so they lay flat on top of each other, right sides outside. Insert the hook through the corresponding stitches or spaces of both layers to crochet them together in the next round.

The tip of the drop shape points to the right. Join **bright yellow** with a standing sc into the first sc next to the ch-2sp (counts as first st).

Round 3: sc 7, sc-inc, [hdc-inc] 4 times, sc-inc, sc 8, °hdc 4° in ch-2sp. (32 sts)

Break the yarn and fasten off invisibly into the stitch after the standing sc from the beginning.

FINISHING AND ASSEMBLING

WINGS

Embroider a **bright yellow** dot onto the front side of the large wings.

Sew the wings into pairs and stitch them onto the belt, left and right of the seam. Finally sew the wing cover into the centre of the wing cluster on the back side. (See Tutorials.)

ANTENNAE

Sew the antennae onto the hat (see Basic Shapes: Antennae).

You're right – yellow doesn't match my complexion. Let's try on the red suit next!

PEACOCK BUTTERFLY (Aglais io)

MATERIALS

HOOK SIZE: US C/2 (2.25mm or 2.5mm)

YARN: Scheepjes Catona 4ply (sport), 100% cotton, 25g/62m – 1 ball of each shade

- 130 Old Lace (off-white)
- 402 Silver Green (light sage)
- 242 Metal Grey (dark grey)
- 388 Rust (red)
- 110 Jet Black (black)
- 101 Candle Light (pale yellow)
- 397 Cyan (blue)

YOU ALSO NEED:

- Toy filling
- 5mm black toy safety eyes

NOTE:

Mark the first stitch of the round with a stitch marker.

Always change to a new yarn in the last step of the last stitch of the old colour (see Tutorials).

PATTERN

HEAD

Using **off white**, follow the top-down head pattern (see Basic Shapes: Head Pattern).

BODY

Using **light sage**, follow the pattern for the plain caterpillar body, type P (see Caterpillar: Body).

HAT

Using **light sage**, follow the hat pattern with standard plain edge (see Basic Shapes: Hat Pattern).

ANTENNAE

Using **dark grey**, follow type A antennae pattern (see Basic Shapes: Antennae).

BELT

Using **dark grey**, follow type A belt pattern (see Basic Shapes: Belt).

WING COVER

Using **dark grey**, follow the wing cover pattern (see Basic Shapes: Wing Cover).

LARGE WINGS

Each wing is made from 2 layers – piece 1 and piece 2 – assembled to become a left or a right large wing.

PIECE 1

Using **red**, make a magic loop (see Tutorials).

Round 1: sc 7 in magic loop. (7 sts)

Round 2: change to **pale yellow**, [sc-inc] 7 times. (14 sts)

Round 3: [sc 1, sc-inc] 3 times, change to **blue**, sc 1, [hdc-inc, hdc 1] 3 times, hdc-inc. (21 sts)

Round 4: change to **black**, sc 1, °hdc 1 + dc 1°, dc 1, dc-inc, dc 1, °dc 1 + hdc 1°, [sc 2, sc-inc] 4 times, sc 3. (28 sts)

Break yarn and close round invisibly into the 2nd stitch of the round (see Tutorials).

Place a marker into the closing stitch.

Start in the closing stitch and count 3 stitches forward. Join **pale yellow** with a standing sc into the 3rd stitch (see Tutorials), then crochet:

Round 5 (part round): sc 1, °sc 1 + hdc 1°, hdc-inc, °hdc 1 + sc 1°, sc 1.

Break yarn and close invisibly.

Join **black** with a standing sc into the 3rd yellow stitch of the last row:

Round 6 (part round): °sc 1 + hdc 1°, hdc 1, °hdc 1 + sc 1°.

Break yarn and close invisibly.

Join **red** with a standing sc into the 2nd yellow stitch of Round 5, sc 1 into the next stitch (the first black one), hdc 1 into the next stitch, then ch 7.

*Crochet into the back bumps on the back side of the chain (see Tutorials). Start in the 2nd back bump from hook: sc 2, hdc 2, dc 2.

Skip 3 black stitches on the margin of the peacock eye and sc 1 into the 4th stitch (this creates a triangle shape in red).

Break yarn and fasten off invisibly.*

Starting in the marked closing stitch of the black 4th round of the peacock eye, count 5 stitches backwards (include the marked stitch as first stitch). Join **red** with a standing slst into the 5th stitch.

Continue in rows.

Row 1: slst 15 evenly along the stitches on the edge, turn (ending at the point of the red triangle).

Row 2: ch 1, slstflo 8, scflo 8, turn.

Row 3: ch 2, skipip st at base of beginning ch-2, hdcblo 7, scblo 6, slstblo 2, turn.

Row 4: ch 1, slstflo 15, turn.

Row 5: ch 2, skip st at base of ch 2, hdcblo 6, scblo 6, slstblo 2, turn.

Row 6: ch 1, slstflo 14.

Break yarn and pull the yarn tail through the last stitch completely.

PIECE 2

Follow pattern for Piece 1 to end Round 3.

Round 4: change to **black**, sc 1, °hdc 1 + dc 1°, dc 1, dc-inc, dc 1, °dc 1 + hdc 1°, sc 3, [sc-inc, sc 2] 4 times. (28 sts)

Break yarn and close round invisibly into the 2nd stitch of the round (see Tutorials).

Place a marker into the closing stitch.

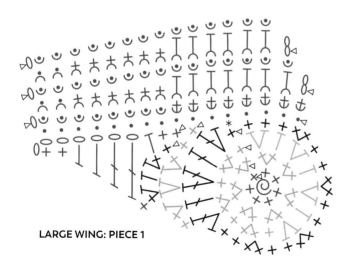

LARGE WING: PIECE 1

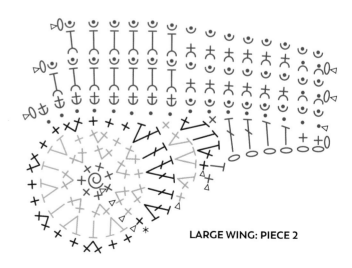

LARGE WING: PIECE 2

Start in the closing stitch and count 4 stitches forward. Join **pale yellow** with a standing sc into the 4th stitch (see Tutorials), then crochet:

Round 5 (part round): °sc 1 + hdc 1°, hdc-inc, °hdc 1 + sc 1°, sc 1.

Break yarn and close invisibly.

Join **black** with a standing sc into the 4th yellow stitch of the last row:

Round 6 (part round): °sc 1 + hdc 1°, hdc 1, °hdc 1 + sc 1°.

Break yarn and close invisibly.

Join **red** with a standing sc into the last yellow stitch before the first black stitch of the last row, hdc 1 into the first black stitch, then ch 7.

Follow pattern for Piece 1 from * to *.

Turn the peacock eye upside down, so the tip of the triangle points to the right. Join **red** with a standing slst into the 1st red stitch on the tip of the triangle:

Continue in rows.

Row 1: slst 15 along the stitches on the edge, turn.

Row 2: ch 1, scflo 8, slstflo 8, turn.

Row 3: ch 1, slstblo 2, scblo 6, hdcblo 7, turn, leaving the last st unworked.

Row 4: ch 1, slstflo 15, turn.

Row 5: ch 1, slstblo 2, scblo 6, hdcblo 6, turn, leaving the last st unworked.

Row 6: ch 1, slstflo 14.

Break yarn and pull the yarn tail through the last stitch completely.

ASSEMBLING 2 PIECES TO MAKE 1 WING

RIGHT WING

Hold piece 2 behind piece 1 so they lay flat on top of each other, right sides outside, with the tip of the red triangle pointing to the right and the peacock eye on the left. Rotate the pieces so the short flat edge of the tip is at the top.

Crochet the stitches of the following round each into both corresponding stitches or spaces on both pieces to connect them.

Join **dark grey** with a standing sc into the end of the first ridge in the right corner of the short flat end: sc 1 into the end of the next 2 ridges, sc 1 into the turning-ch on the tip of the little red triangle. (4 sts)

Rotate 90 degrees and work along the next side of the wing: hdc 18.

Rotate 90 degrees to work along the next edge: dc-inc, °dc 1 + ch 2 + slst 1 into 2nd ch from hook + dc 1°, dc-inc, hdc 4, skip 1.

Crochet a shell of °dc 1 + hdc 3° into the same black stitch as the first red slst was already worked into, sc 1 into the end of the first ridge.

Work the next shell into the space between the first and the second ridge. Insert hook into the space under the corresponding ch-2 space/and the last hdc and work a shell of °hdc 4° in there, sc 1 into the end of the second ridge.

Place another shell of °hdc 3 + dc 1° into the last space under the last hdc/and ch-2 space between the second and the last ridge.

Rotate 90 degrees and crochet along the bottom side of the wing: sc 14.

Rotate 90 degrees and work along the short flat end again: °slst 1 + ch 3 + dc 1° into the 1st st, hdc 1, sc 1, sc-inc.

Break the yarn and close the round invisibly. Weave in all ends.

LEFT WING

Hold piece 1 behind piece 2 so they lay flat on top of each other, right sides outside, with the tip of the red triangle points to the left and the peacock eye on the right. Rotate the pieces so the short flat edge of the tip is at the top.

Crochet the stitches of the following round each into both corresponding stitches or spaces on both pieces to connect them.

Join **dark grey** with a standing sc into the turning-ch on the tip of the little red triangle: sc 1 into the end of the next 3 ridges. (4 sts)

Rotate 90 degrees and work along the next side of the wing: sc 14.

Rotate 90 degrees to work along the next edge, insert hook into the space between the first and the second ridge under the last hdc of the row/or the corresponding ch-2 space, and work a shell of °dc 1 + hdc 3° in there.

Sc 1 into the turning chain at the end of the middle ridge. Crochet another shell of °hdc 4° into the next space between the 2nd and the last ridge (insert hook under the last hdc/or ch-2), sc 1 into the turning chain at the end of the last ridge.

Place another shell of °hdc 3 + dc 1° into the same black stitch as the last red one was already worked into.

Skip 1 black stitch, hdc 4, dc-inc, °dc 1 + ch 2 + slst 1 into 2nd ch from hook + dc 1°, rotate 90 degrees and crochet on along the margin: dc-inc, hdc 18.

Rotate 90 degrees and work along the short flat end again: °sc-inc°, sc 1, hdc 1, dc 1, ch 3, slst in next stitch.

Break the yarn.

The spots on the peacock butterfly's wings imitate big eyes to scare away predators.

SMALL WINGS

Each wing is made from 2 layers – piece 1 and piece 2 – assembled to become a left or a right small wing.

PIECE 1

Using **blue**, make a magic loop (see Tutorials).

Round 1: sc 6 into magic loop. (6 sts)

Round 2: change to **black**, sc-inc in every st. (12 sts)

Round 3: sc 1, change to **pale yellow**, [sc-inc, sc 1] 5 times, sc-inc. (18 sts)

Round 4 (part round): sc 2, change to **black**: sc 1, hdc-inc, sc 1.

Break yarn and close invisibly.

Round 5: Join **red** with a standing sc into the 1st black stitch of last round, ch 5, crochet into the back bumps on the back side of the chain. Start in the 2nd back bump from hook: sc 1, hdc 1, dc 1, tr 1, skip 2 black stitches on the edge of the peacock eye and sc 1 into the next st, sc 2, [sc 2, sc-inc] 4 times, sc 1.

Round 6: slst in 1st stitch, slst 4.

Break yarn and fasten off invisibly into the 1st stitch on the other side of the tip. Weave in all ends.

PIECE 2

Follow pattern for Piece 1 to end Round 4. Break yarn and close invisibly.

Round 5: Join **red** with a standing sc into the 2nd black stitch of last round, ch 5, crochet into the back bumps on the back side of the chain. Start in the 2nd back bump from hook: sc 1, hdc 1, dc 1, tr 1, skip 2 black stitches on the edge of the peacock eye and sc 1 into the next st, sc 1, [sc-inc, sc 2] 4 times, sc 2.

Round 6: slst in 1st stitch, slst 4.

Break yarn and fasten off invisibly into the 1st stitch on the other side of the tip. Weave in all ends.

ASSEMBLING 2 PIECES TO MAKE 1 WING

RIGHT WING

Hold piece 2 behind piece 1 so they lay flat on top of each other, right sides outside, so that the tip points to the right. Crochet together the corresponding stitches of both layers with the following stitches.

Join **dark grey** with a standing sc into the 1st stitch next to the closing stitch on the tip of the little red triangle: sc 3, [sc-inc, sc 1] 3 times, °sc 1 + hdc 1°, [skip 1, °hdc 4°, slst 1] twice, sc 1, hdc 1, ch 2, sc into 2nd ch from hook, sc into next stitch along edge, sc 10.

Break the yarn and close the round invisibly into the first stitch of the round.

SMALL WING: PIECE 1

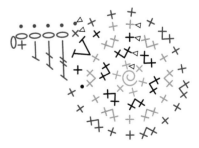

SMALL WING: PIECE 2

LEFT WING

Hold piece 1 behind piece 2 so they lay flat on top of each other, right sides outside, so that the tip points to the left.

Rotate the pieces 180° to start along what will become the bottom side of the wing. Crochet together the corresponding stitches of both layers with the following stitches.

Join **dark grey** with a standing sc into the 1st stitch next to the closing stitch on the tip of the little red triangle: sc 10, ch 2, sc into 2nd ch from hook, hdc 1 into next stitch along the edge, sc 1, [slst 1, °hdc 4°, skip 1] twice, °hdc 1 + sc 1°, [sc 1, sc-inc] 3 times, sc 4.

Break the yarn and close the round invisibly into the first stitch of the round.

ASSEMBLING

WINGS

Sew the wings into pairs and stitch them onto the belt, left and right of the seam. Finally sew the wing cover into the centre of the wing cluster on the back side. (See Tutorials: Assembling Butterfly Wings.)

ANTENNAE

Sew the antennae onto the hat (see Basic Shapes: Antennae).

ULYSSES BUTTERFLY (Papilio ulysses)

MATERIALS

HOOK SIZE: US C/2 (2.25mm or 2.5mm)

YARN: Scheepjes Catona 4ply (sport), 100% cotton, 25g/62m – 1 ball of each shade:

- 130 Old Lace (off-white)
- 242 Metal Grey (dark grey)
- 397 Cyan (blue)
- 110 Jet Black (black)

YOU ALSO NEED:

- Toy filling
- 5mm black toy safety eyes

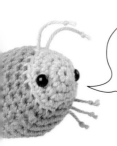

Butterfly wings are covered with countless colourful scales.

PATTERN

HEAD

Using **off white**, follow the top-down head pattern (see Basic Shapes: Head Pattern).

BODY

Using **dark grey** and **black**, follow the pattern for the wide striped caterpillar body, type S2 (see Caterpillar: Body).

HAT

Using **black**, follow the hat pattern with standard plain edge (see Basic Shapes: Hat Pattern).

ANTENNAE

Using **black**, follow type A antennae pattern (see Basic Shapes: Antennae).

BELT

Using **black**, follow type A belt pattern (see Basic Shapes: Belt).

WING COVER

Using **black**, follow the wing cover pattern (see Basic Shapes: Wing Cover).

LARGE WINGS

Each wing is made from 2 layers – piece 1 and piece 2 – assembled to become a left or a right wing. Make pieces 1 and 2, then assemble them to become 1 wing, before you work the next 2 pieces for the second wing.

NOTES FOR WINGS:

The first stitch to work into at the beginning of a new row is the stitch at the base of the turning chain.

On rows ending with dc stitches, the last stitch of a row is always worked into the top of the beginning ch-3 from the previous row (this is the 3rd ch counting from the bottom).

Ch 1 at the beginning of a row does not count as a stitch.

PIECE 1

Using **blue**, ch 13.

Start in the 4th ch from hook:

Row 1: dc-inc, dc 1, hdc 4, sc 4, turn. (11 sts)

Row 2: ch 1, sc 4, hdc 4, dc 4, turn. (12 sts)

Row 3: ch 3, dc-inc into st at base of beginning ch-3, dc 3, hdc 5, sc 3, turn. (13 sts)

Row 4: ch 1, sc 3, hdc 5, dc 6, turn. (14 sts)

Row 5: ch 3, dc-inc into st at base of beginning ch-3, dc 5, hdc 6, sc 2, turn. (15 sts)

Row 6: ch 1, sc 2, hdc 6, dc 8. (16 sts)

Break yarn and fasten off.

PIECE 2

Using **blue**, ch 11.

Start in the 2nd ch from hook:

Row 1: sc 4, hdc 4, dc 1, dc-inc, turn. (11 sts)

Row 2: ch 3, dc-inc into st at base of beginning ch-3, dc 2, hdc 4, sc 4, turn. (12 sts)

Row 3: ch 1, sc 3, hdc 5, dc 5, turn. (13 sts)

Row 4: ch 3, dc-inc into st at the base of beginning ch-3, dc 4, hdc 5, sc 3, turn. (14 sts)

Row 5: ch 1, sc 2, hdc 6, dc 7, turn. (15 sts)

Row 6: ch 3, dc-inc into st at base of beginning ch-3, dc 6, hdc 6, sc 2. (16 sts)

Do not break yarn.

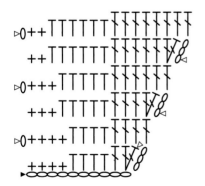

LARGE WING: PIECE 1

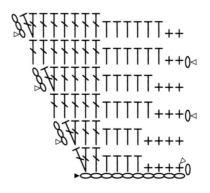

LARGE WING: PIECE 2

With each flap, a butterfly loses hundreds of scales, so its colours dull.

ASSEMBLING PIECES 1 AND 2 TO MAKE 1 LARGE WING

Hold piece 1 behind piece 2 so they lay flat on top of each other, right sides outside, the short end of the wing points to the left.

Rotate 90 degrees clockwise. Now the short end of the wing is at the top and the working stitch is in the top right corner.

For Row 1, insert the hook through the corresponding stitches or spaces of both layers to crochet them together as follows:

Row 1: ch 1, sc 1 into the same stitch as the last sc in Row 6, sc 4 across the ends of the rows along the short end, turn. (5 sts)

Row 2: ch 1, sc2tog, sc 1, sc2tog, turn. (3 sts)

Row 3: ch 1, sc 1, sc2tog. (2 sts)

Break the yarn and weave in all ends.

LEFT WING

With right side still facing, the long upper side of the wing is still on the right and the short end of the wing is still facing you, join **black** with a standing sc into the first stitch of previous Row 3 in the right corner of the short end: °sc 1 + ch 1 + sc 1° into the second stitch – rotate 90 degrees clockwise.

Crochet along the bottom edge of the wing: sc 2 into the ends of the rows that build the tip. Working through both layers: sc 10 along the remaining loops of the foundation chains, rotate 90 degrees clockwise.

Crochet along the tall side of the wing. Work into the ch-3sp and/or post of the dc on the end of each row: ch 1, °sc 3° into the first and second space, °hdc 3° into the 3rd, 4th and 5th space, °dc 3 + ch 1 + dc 2° into the last space, rotate 90 degrees clockwise.

Crochet along the upper edge of the wing: dc 3, hdc 2, sc 11, sc 2 across the ends of the blue rows, sc 1 into same stitch as beginning join.

Break the yarn and close invisibly into the first stitch of the round.

RIGHT WING

Turn piece, so the long upper edge of the wing is on the left and the short end is the top edge. Join **black** with a standing sc into the last stitch of previous Row 3 in the right corner of the short end: °sc 1 + ch 1 + sc 1° into the second stitch – rotate 90 degrees clockwise.

Crochet along the next side of the wing: sc 2 into the ends of the rows that build the tip. Working through both layers: sc 11, hdc 2, dc 3, rotate 90 degrees clockwise.

Crochet along the tall side of the wing. Work into ch-3sp and/or post of the dc on the end of each row: °dc 2 + ch 1 + dc 3° into the first space, °hdc 3° into the 2nd, 3rd and 4th space, °sc 3° into 5th and last space, rotate 90 degrees clockwise.

Crochet along the bottom edge of the wing: ch 1, sc 10 into the remaining loops from the foundation chain, sc 2 across the ends of the blue rows, sc 1 into same stitch as beginning join.

Break the yarn and close invisibly into the first stitch of the round.

SMALL WINGS

Each wing is made from 2 layers – piece 1 and piece 2 – assembled to become a left or a right wing. Make piece 1 and piece 2, then assemble them to become 1 wing, before you work the next 2 pieces for the second wing. Refer to notes for wings.

PIECE 1

Using **blue**, ch 8.

Start in 2nd ch from hook:

Row 1: sc 2, hdc 3, dc 1, dc-inc, turn. (8 sts)

Row 2: ch 3, dc 3, hdc 3, sc 2, turn. (9 sts)

Row 3: ch 1, sc 2, hdc 3, dc 4.

Break yarn, fasten off and weave in the ends on the wrong side.

PIECE 2

Using **blue**, ch 10.

Start in 4th ch from hook:

Row 1: dc-inc, dc 1, hdc 3, sc 2, turn. (8 sts)

Row 2: ch 1, sc 2, hdc 3, dc 4, turn. (9 sts)

Row 3: ch 3, dc 4, hdc 3, sc 2.

Break yarn, fasten off and weave in the ends on the wrong side.

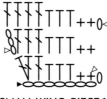

SMALL WING: PIECE 1

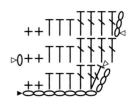

SMALL WING: PIECE 2

ASSEMBLING PIECE 1 AND PIECE 2 TO MAKE 1 SMALL WING

To join layers to become 1 wing, insert the hook through the corresponding stitches on both layers to crochet them together with the following round:

RIGHT WING

Hold piece 2 behind piece 1 so they lay flat on top of each other, right sides outside, the short end of the wing points to the right, the upper side of the wing is the top edge.

Join **black** with a standing sc into the first pair of stitches on the upper side of the wing (top right corner): sc 5 along edge, hdc 2, hdc-inc, rotate 90 degrees clockwise, now the tall side of the wing is facing you.

Work into the space underneath the last dc and/or turning chain at the end of a row: °hdc 2 + dc 1° into the first space, ch-1picot, °dc 2, ch-1picot, dc 2° into second space, ch-1picot, °dc 2° into the third space, ch 8, now crochet into the bumps on the back of the chain (see Tutorials): dc-inc into the 3rd back bump from hook, hdc 2, sc 1, slst 2, then °dc 1 + hdc 1° into the same space as the first two hdc's, rotate 90 degrees clockwise.

Crochet into the remaining loops of the foundation chains on the bottom side of the wing: hdc 2, sc 5, rotate 90 degrees clockwise.

The short end is at the top. Find the end of the row in the centre of the short side of the wing and crochet the following cluster of stitches into it: °hdc 2 + dc 1 + ch 1 + dc 1 + hdc 2°.

Break the yarn and close the row invisibly into the standing sc from the beginning of the round.

LEFT WING

Hold piece 1 behind piece 2 so they lay flat on top of each other, right sides outside, short end of the wing points right, bottom edge of the wing is top edge.

Join **black** with a standing sc into the first pair of remaining loops from the foundation chains on the bottom side (these are at the top right corner): sc 4, hdc 2 along the bottom edge, rotate 90 degrees clockwise, now the tall side of the wing is at the top.

Work into the space underneath the last dc and/or turning chain at the end of a row: °hdc 1 + dc 1° into the first space, ch 8, now crochet into the bumps on the back of the chain: dc-inc into the 3rd back bump from hook, hdc 2, sc 1, slst 2, then °dc 2° into the same space as the dc + hdc, ch-1picot, °dc 2, ch-1picot, dc 2° into second space, ch-1picot, °dc 1 + hdc 2° into the last space.

Rotate 90 degrees clockwise, so the top side of the wing is up and facing you: hdc-inc, hdc 2, sc 6, rotate 90 degrees clockwise.

The short end is facing you. Find the end of the row in the very centre of the short side of the wing and crochet the following cluster of stitches into there: °hdc 2 + dc 1 + ch 1 + dc 1 + hdc 2°.

Break the yarn and close the row invisibly into the standing sc from the beginning of the round.

ASSEMBLING

WINGS

Sew the wings into pairs and stitch them onto the belt, left and right of the seam. Finally, sew the wing cover into the centre of the wing cluster on the back side. (See Tutorials).

ANTENNAE

Sew the antennae onto the hat (see Basic Shapes: Antennae).

GOLDEN DAYDREAM MOTH

(Somniatrix diurna lalylalensis)

MATERIALS

HOOK SIZE: US C/2 (2.5mm or 2.25mm)

YARN: Scheepjes Catona 4ply (sport), 100% cotton, 25g/62m – 1 ball of each shade:

- 130 Old Lace (off-white)
- 383 Ginger Gold (golden brown)
- 179 Topaz (camel)
- 172 Light Silver (silver grey)
- 402 Silver Green (light sage)
- 401 Teal (emerald)

YOU ALSO NEED:

- Toy filling
- 5mm black toy safety eyes

PATTERN

HEAD

Using **off white**, follow the top-down head pattern (see Basic Shapes: Head Pattern).

BODY

Using **camel**, follow the pattern for the plain caterpillar body, type P (see Caterpillar: Body).

HAT

Using **golden brown**, follow the hat pattern with standard plain edge (see Basic Shapes: Hat Pattern).

ANTENNAE

Using **camel**, follow type B antennae pattern (see Basic Shapes: Antennae).

BELT

Using **off-white**, follow type A belt pattern (see Basic Shapes: Belt).

Carefully brush the surface of the fabric with a soft wire brush to make the belt look fuzzy.

WING COVER

Using **emerald**, follow the wing cover pattern (see Basic Shapes: Wing Cover).

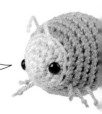

This extremely rare species can only be found in Lalylaland.

LARGE WINGS

Each wing is made from 2 layers – piece 1 and piece 2 – assembled to become a left or a right wing. Make pieces 1 and 2, then assemble them to become 1 wing, before you work the next 2 pieces for the second wing.

NOTES FOR WING PIECES 1 AND 2:

The first stitch to work into at the beginning of a new row is the stitch at the base of the turning chain.

On rows ending with dc stitches, the last stitch of a row is always worked into the top of the beginning ch-3 from the previous row (this is the 3rd ch counting from the bottom).

PIECE 1

Using **off-white**, ch 13.

Start in the 4th ch from hook:

Row 1: dc-inc, dc 1, hdc 4, sc 4, turn. (11 sts)

Row 2: ch 1, sc 4, hdc 4, dc 4, turn. (12 sts)

Row 3: ch 3, dc-inc into st at base of beginning ch-3, dc 3, hdc 5, sc 3, turn. (13 sts)

Row 4: ch 1, sc 3, hdc 5, dc 6, turn. (14 sts)

Row 5: ch 3, dc-inc into st at base of beginning ch-3, dc 5, hdc 6, sc 2, turn. (15 sts)

Row 6: ch 1, sc 2, hdc 6, dc 8. (16 sts)

Break yarn and fasten off.

PIECE 2

Using **off-white**, ch 11.

Start in the 2nd ch from hook:

Row 1: sc 4, hdc 4, dc 1, dc-inc, turn. (11 sts)

Row 2: ch 3, dc-inc into st at base of beginning ch-3, dc 2, hdc 4, sc 4, turn. (12 sts)

Row 3: ch 1, sc 3, hdc 5, dc 5, turn. (13 sts)

Row 4: ch 3, dc-inc into st at the base of beginning ch-3, dc 4, hdc 5, sc 3, turn. (14 sts)

Row 5: ch 1, sc 2, hdc 6, dc 7, turn. (15 sts)

Row 6: ch 3, dc-inc into st at base of beginning ch-3, dc 6, hdc 6, sc 2, turn. (16 sts)

Do not break yarn.

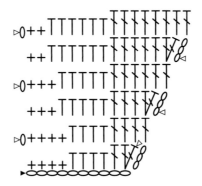

LARGE WING: PIECE 1

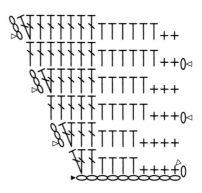

LARGE WING: PIECE 2

ASSEMBLING PIECES 1 AND 2 TO MAKE 1 WING

Hold piece 1 behind piece 2 so they lay flat on top of each other, right sides outside, the short end of the wing points to the left.

Rotate 90 degrees clockwise. Now the short end of the wing is at the top and the working stitch is in the top right corner.

Insert the hook through the corresponding stitches or spaces of both layers to crochet them together as follows: ch 1, sc 1 into the same stitch as the last sc in Row 6, sc 4 across the ends of the rows along the short end. (5 sts)

Break the yarn and weave in all ends on the wrong side of the fabric.

LEFT WING

With right side still facing, join **silver grey** with a standing sc into the first stitch of the previous row in the right corner of the short end (this counts as 1st stitch).

Row 1: 4 sc, turn. (5 sts)

Row 2: ch 1 (not counted as a st here and throughout), sc2tog, sc 1, sc2tog, turn. (3 sts)

Row 3: ch 1, sc 1, sc2tog, rotate 90 degrees clockwise. (2 sts)

Crochet along the bottom edge of the wing: ch 1, sc 3 across the ends of the **silver grey** rows, insert the hook through the corresponding stitches of both layers, sc 10 along the remaining loops of the foundation chains, rotate 90 degrees clockwise.

Crochet along the long side of the wing: ch 1, [°sc 3° into the next ch-3 sp and/or post of the dc on the end of each row] 6 times. rotate 90 degrees clockwise.

Crochet along the upper edge of the wing: ch 1, sc 16, sc 3 across the ends of the **silver grey** rows.

Break the yarn and close invisibly into the first stitch of the round.

RIGHT WING

With the wrong side of the last row facing and the upper side of the wing on the left, join **silver grey** with a standing sc into the first stitch in the right corner of the short end (this is the last stitch of the previous row and this counts as 1st stitch).

Row 1: 4 sc, turn. (5 sts)

Row 2: ch 1 (not counted as a st here and throughout), sc2tog, sc 1, sc2tog, turn. (3 sts)

Row 3: ch 1, sc2tog, sc 1, rotate 90 degrees clockwise. (2 sts)

Crochet along the upper edge of the wing: ch 1, sc 3 across the ends of the **silver grey** rows, insert the hook through the corresponding stitches of both layers, sc 16, rotate 90 degrees clockwise.

Continue along the long side of the wing: ch 1, [°sc 3° into the next ch-3 sp and/or post of the dc on the end of each row] 6 times, rotate 90 degrees clockwise.

Crochet along the bottom edge of the wing: ch 1, sc 10 into the remaining loops from the foundation chains, sc 3 across the ends of the **silver grey** rows.

Break the yarn and close invisibly into the first stitch of the round.

SMALL WINGS

Each wing is made from 2 layers – piece 1 and piece 2 – assembled to become a left or a right wing. Refer to notes for wing pieces 1 and 2.

PIECE 1

Using **light sage**, ch 8.

Start in the 2nd ch from hook:

Row 1: sc 2, hdc 3, dc 1, dc-inc, turn. (8 sts)

Row 2: ch 3, dc 3, hdc 3, sc 2, turn. (9 sts)

Row 3: ch 1, sc 2, hdc 3, dc 4.

Break yarn, fasten off and weave in the ends on the wrong side

PIECE 2

Using **light sage**, ch 10.

Start in the 4th ch from hook:

Row 1: dc-inc, dc 1, hdc 3, sc 2, turn. (8 sts)

Row 2: ch 1, sc 2, hdc 3, dc 4, turn. (9 sts)

Row 3: ch 3, dc 4, hdc 3, sc 2.

Break yarn, fasten off and weave in the ends on the wrong side.

ASSEMBLING PIECES 1 AND 2 TO MAKE 1 WING

To join both layers to become 1 wing, insert the hook through the corresponding stitches on both layers to crochet them together.

RIGHT WING

Hold piece 2 behind piece 1 so they lay flat on top of each other, right sides outside, the short end of the wing points to the right, the upper side of the wing is the top edge.

Join **light sage** with a standing sc into the first pair of stitches on the upper side of the wing (top right corner): sc 8 along the upper edge, rotate 90 degrees clockwise – now the tall end of the wing is at the top.

Work into the space underneath the last dc and/or turning chain at the end of a row: ch 1, [°sc 3° into each space] 3 times, rotate 90 degrees clockwise.

Crochet into the remaining loops of the foundation chains on the bottom side of the wing: ch 1, sc 7, rotate 90 degrees clockwise.

The short end is at the top. Crochet the following cluster of stitches into the end of the row in the very centre of the short side: °hdc 2 + dc 1 + ch 1 + dc 1 + hdc 2°.

Break the yarn and close the row invisibly into the standing sc from the beginning of the round.

LEFT WING

Hold piece 1 behind piece 2 so they lay flat on top of each other, right sides outside, the short end of the wing points to the right, bottom edge of the wing is the top edge.

Join **light sage** with a standing sc into the first pair of remaining loops from the foundation chains on the bottom side (these are at the top right corner): sc 7 into remaining loops on initial foundation chains, rotate 90 degrees clockwise – now the tall end of the wing is at the top.

Work into the space underneath the last dc and/or turning chain at the end of a row: ch 1, [°sc 3° into each space] 3 times, rotate 90 degrees clockwise.

Crochet along the upper side of the wing: ch 1, sc 9, rotate 90 degrees clockwise.

The short end is facing you. Crochet the following cluster of stitches into the end of the row in the very centre of the short side: °hdc 2 + dc 1 + ch 1 + dc 1 + hdc 2°.

Break the yarn and close the row invisibly into the standing sc from the beginning of the round.

ASSEMBLING

WINGS

Sew the wings into pairs and stitch them onto the belt, left and right of the seam. Finally, sew the wing cover into the centre of the wing cluster on the back side. (See Tutorials).

ANTENNAE

Sew the antennae onto the hat (see Basic Shapes: Antennae).

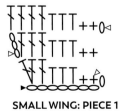

SMALL WING: PIECE 1

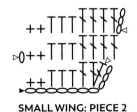

SMALL WING: PIECE 2

BEETLE LARVA

MATERIALS:

HOOK SIZE: US C/2 (2.5mm or 2.25mm)

YARN: Scheepjes Catona 4ply (sport), 100% cotton, 25g/62m – 1 ball of each shade

Ladybird
· 130 Old Lace (off white)
· 393 Charcoal (dark grey)
· 281 Royal Orange (orange)

Stag beetle
· 130 Old Lace (off white)
· 383 Ginger Gold (golden brown)
· 162 Black Coffee (dark brown)

YOU ALSO NEED:
· Toy filling
· 5mm black toy safety eyes

PATTERN

HEAD

Using **off-white**, follow the top-down-version of the head to the end of Round 16 (see Basic Shapes: Head Pattern). Change to the colour for the body (**dark grey** for the ladybird and **golden brown** for the stag beetle) in the last step of the last stitch for the head.

BODY

Round 17: slst 21.

Round 18: scblo 21.

Rounds 19–20: sc 21 (2 rounds).

Round 21: slst 21.

Round 22: scflo 1, scflo-inc, [scflo 2, scflo-inc] 6 times, scflo 1. (28 sts)

Round 23: sc 28.

Round 24: [sc 6, sc-inc] 4 times. (32 sts)

Rounds 25–29: sc 32 (5 rounds).

Round 30: [sc2tog, sc 6] 4 times. (28 sts)

Round 31: sc 28.

Round 32: sc 1, sc2tog, [sc 2, sc2tog] 6 times, sc 1. (21 sts)

Round 33: sc 21.

Stuff the body firmly.

Round 34: [sc2tog, sc 1] 7 times. (14 sts)

Round 35: [sc2tog] 7 times. (7 sts)

Stuff a little more, then break the yarn. Close the remaining stitches through the front loops (see Tutorials) and weave in all yarn tails.

HAT

Using **dark grey** for the ladybird and **dark brown** for the stag beetle, follow the hat pattern with standard plain edge (see Basic Shapes: Hat Pattern).

FINISHING

LADYBIRD

Using **orange**, embroider 4 spots in a 2 x 2 cluster onto the larva's back.

No, not cute! These beasts each gobble thousands of my friends!

BEETLE PUPA

MATERIALS:

HOOK SIZE: US C/2 (2.5mm or 2.25mm)

YARN: Scheepjes Catona 4ply (sport), 100% cotton, 25g/62m – 1 ball of each shade

- 281 Tangerine or 411 Sweet Orange (orange)
- 110 Jet Black (black)

PATTERN

CIRCLES (MAKE 2)

Using **black**, make a magic loop (see Tutorials).

Round 1: ch 2 (not counted as a st), hdc 12 into magic loop. (12 sts)

Tighten the loop, break the yarn and fasten off invisibly (see Tutorials) into the top of the first hdc (13 sts remain in the circle).

CASE

Take one of the circles (with wrong side facing you) and join the **orange** yarn with a slip knot through any stitch (see Tutorials), ch 15. Take the second circle (with right side facing you) and sc 1 into any stitch.

Turn your work and crochet the following row into the back loops along the chain:

Row 1: skip 1st stitch from hook, slstblo 2, scblo 10, slstblo 2, connect the row to the first circle by working sc 1 into the same place as the initial join on the circle's edge (see photo 1), turn. (15 sts)

Row 2: skip 1st stitch, slstblo 2, scblo 4, [scblo-inc] twice, scblo 4, slstblo 2, sc 1 into the same stitch as you've joined the second circle, turn. (17 sts)

Row 3: skip 1st stitch, slstblo 2, scblo 12, slstblo 2, sc 1 into 2nd stitch on first circle, turn.

NOTE:

Crochet all stitches of every row through back loops only (see photo 2).

You will be working 2 orange stitches into each stitch on the edge of the black circles.

Work into both loops when joining to the stitches on the edge of the circles.

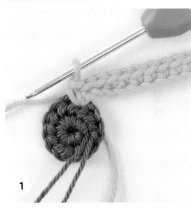

1

2

101

Row 4: skip 1st stitch, slstblo 2, scblo 4, hdcblo 1, [hdcblo-inc] twice, hdcblo 1, scblo 4, slstblo 2, sc 1 into 2nd stitch on second circle, turn. (19 sts)

Row 5: skip 1st stitch, slstblo 2, scblo 14, slstblo 2, sc 1 into 2nd stitch on first circle, turn. (19 sts)

Row 6: skip 1st stitch, slstblo 2, scblo 4, hdcblo 2, [hdcblo 2] twice, hdcblo 2, scblo 4, slstblo 2, sc 1 into 2nd stitch on second circle, turn. (21 sts)

Row 7: skip 1st stitch, slstblo 2, scblo 16, slstblo 2, sc 1 into 3rd stitch on first circle, turn.

Row 8: skip 1st stitch, slstblo 2, scblo 4, hdcblo 3, [hdcblo 2] twice, hdcblo 3, scblo 4, slstblo 2, sc 1 into 3rd stitch on second circle, turn. (23 sts)

Row 9: skip 1st stitch, slstblo 2, scblo 18, slstblo 2, sc 1 into 3rd stitch on the first circle, turn.

Row 10: skip 1st stitch, slstblo 2, scblo 3, hdcblo 3, dcblo 2, [dcblo-inc] twice, dcblo 2, hdcblo 3, scblo 3, slstblo 2, sc 1 into 3rd stitch on second circle, turn. (25 sts)

Row 11: skip 1st stitch, slstblo 2, scblo 20, slstblo 2, sc 1 into the 4th stitch on the first circle, turn.

Row 12: skip 1st stitch, slstblo 2, scblo 3, hdcblo 3, dcblo 3, [trblo-inc] twice, dcblo 3, hdcblo 3, scblo 3, slstblo 2, sc 1 into 4th stitch on second circle, turn. (27 sts)

Row 13: skip 1st stitch, slstblo 2, scblo 22, slstblo 2, sc 1 into 4th stitch on the first circle, turn.

Row 14: skip 1st stitch, slstblo 2, scblo 3, hdcblo 3, dcblo 4, [trblo-inc] twice, dcblo 4, hdcblo 3, scblo 3, slstblo 2, sc 1 into the 4th stitch on the second circle, turn. (29 sts)

Row 15: skip 1st stitch, slstblo 2, scblo 24, slstblo 2, sc 1 into the 5th stitch on the first circle, turn.

Row 16: skip 1st stitch, slstblo 2, scblo 3, hdcblo 3, dcblo 4, trblo 4, dcblo 4, hdcblo 3, scblo 3, slstblo 2, sc 1 into the 5th stitch on second circle, turn.

Row 17: skip 1st stitch, slstblo 2, scblo 24, slstblo 2, sc 1 into the 5th stitch on the first circle, turn.

Row 18: skip 1st stitch, slstblo 2, scblo 3, hdcblo 3, dcblo 3, trblo 1, [tr2tog-blo] twice, trblo 1, dcblo 3, hdcblo 3, scblo 3, slstblo 2, sc 1 into the 5th stitch on second circle, turn. (27 sts)

Row 19: skip 1st stitch, slstblo 2, scblo 22, slstblo 2, sc 1 into the 6th stitch on the first circle, turn.

Row 20: skip 1st stitch, slstblo 2, scblo 3, hdcblo 3, dcblo 2, [dc2tog-blo, dcblo 2] twice, hdcblo 3, scblo 3, slstblo 2, sc 1 into the 6th stitch on second circle, turn. (25 sts)

Row 21: skip 1st stitch, slstblo 2, scblo 20, slstblo 2, sc 1 into the 6th stitch on first circle, turn.

Row 22: skip 1st stitch, slstblo 2, scblo 3, hdcblo 3, dcblo 1, dc2tog-blo, dcblo 2, dc2tog-blo, dcblo 1, hdcblo 3, scblo 3, slstblo 2, sc 1 into the 6th stitch on second circle, turn. (23 sts)

Row 23: skip 1st stitch, slstblo 2, scblo 18, slstblo 2, sc 1 into the 7th stitch on the first circle, turn.

Row 24: skip 1st stitch, slstblo 2, scblo 3, hdcblo 3, dcblo 6, hdcblo 3, scblo 3, slstblo 2, sc 1 into the 7th stitch on second circle, turn.

Row 25: repeat Row 23.

Row 26: repeat Row 24.

Row 27: repeat Row 23, but sc 1 into 8th stitch on first circle, turn.

Row 28: repeat Row 24, but sc 1 into 8th stitch on second circle, turn.

Row 29: repeat Row 27.

Row 30: skip 1st stitch, slstblo 2, scblo 3, hdcblo 3, dcblo 2, [dcblo-inc] twice, dcblo 2, hdcblo 3, scblo 3, slstblo 2, sc 1 into the 8th stitch on second circle, turn. (25 sts)

Row 31: skip 1st stitch, slstblo 2, scblo 20, slstblo 2, sc 1 into the 9th stitch on the first circle, turn.

Row 32: skip 1st stitch, slstblo 2, scblo 3, hdcblo 3, dcblo 3, [trblo-inc] twice, dcblo 3, hdcblo 3, scblo 3, slstblo 2, sc 1 into the 9th stitch on second circle, turn. (27 sts)

Row 33: skip 1st stitch, slstblo 2, scblo 22, slstblo 2, sc 1 into the 9th stitch on the first circle, turn.

Row 34: skip 1st stitch, slstblo 2, scblo 3, hdcblo 3, dcblo 3, trblo 1, [trblo-inc] twice, trblo 1, dcblo 3, hdcblo 3, scblo 3, slstblo 2, sc 1 into the 9th stitch on second circle, turn. (29 sts)

Row 35: skip 1st stitch, slstblo 2, scblo 24, slstblo 2, sc 1 into the 10th stitch on the first circle, turn.

Row 36: skip 1st stitch, slstblo 2, scblo 3, hdcblo 3, dcblo 3, trblo 2, [trblo-inc] twice, trblo 2, dcblo 3, hdcblo 3, scblo 3, slstblo 2, sc 1 into the 10th stitch on second circle, turn. (31 sts)

Row 37: skip 1st stitch, slstblo 2, scblo 26, slstblo 2, sc 1 into the 10th stitch on the first circle, turn.

Row 38: skip 1st stitch, slstblo 2, scblo 3, hdcblo 3, dcblo 3, trblo 3, [trblo-inc] twice, trblo 3, dcblo 3, hdcblo 3, scblo 3, slstblo 2, sc 1 into the 10th stitch on the second circle, turn. (33 sts)

Row 39: skip 1st stitch, slstblo 2, scblo 28, slstblo 2, sc 1 into the 11th stitch on the first circle, turn.

Row 40: skip 1st stitch, slstblo 2, scblo 3, hdcblo 3, dcblo 4, trblo 3, [trblo-inc] twice, trblo 3, dcblo 4, hdcblo 3, scblo 3, slstblo 2, sc 1 into the 11th stitch on second circle, turn. (35 sts)

Row 41: skip 1st stitch, slstblo 2, scblo 30, slstblo 2, sc 1 into the 11th stitch on the first circle, turn.

Row 42: skip 1st stitch, slst 2, sc 4, hdc 5, dc 12, hdc 5, sc 4, slst 2, sc 1 into the 11th stitch on second circle, turn.

Row 43: skip 1st stitch, slstblo 2, scblo 30, slstblo 2, sc 1 into the 12th stitch on the first circle, turn.

Row 44: skip 1st stitch, slstblo 2, scblo 5, hdcblo 5, dcblo 10, hdcblo 5, scblo 5, slstblo 2, sc 1 into the 12th stitch on the second circle, **do not** turn and **do not** break the yarn.

FINISHING

To get a tidy border around the open end of the pupa, crochet a round of slip stitches all across every stitch along the edge, working under both loops of the stitches: sc 1 into the last remaining stitch on the edge of the circle, slst 1 in each of the remaining loops from the foundation chain, sc 1 into the remaining 13th stitch on the edge of the other circle, slst 34 along the stitches of the 44th row.

Break the yarn and fasten off invisibly (see Tutorials). Weave in all ends.

LADYBIRD (Coccinellidae)

MATERIALS

HOOK SIZE: US C/2 (2.5mm or 2.25mm)

YARN: Scheepjes Catona 4ply (sport), 100% cotton, 25g/62m –1 ball of each shade

- 130 Old Lace (off white)
- 393 Charcoal (dark grey)
- 390 Poppy Rose (red)
- 110 Jet Black (black)

YOU ALSO NEED:

- Toy filling
- 5mm black toy safety eyes

PATTERN

HEAD

Using **off-white**, follow the top-down head pattern (see Basic Shapes: Head Pattern).

BODY

Using **dark grey,** follow the beetle larva body pattern (see Beetle Larva).

HAT

Using **black**, follow the hat pattern with pointy beetle edge (see Basic Shapes: Hat Pattern).

ANTENNAE

Using **black**, follow type A antennae pattern (see Basic Shapes: Antennae).

WING SUIT

The wing suit is made by crocheting 2 separate wing layers, 1 in red and 1 in off-white. These are assembled into one piece before working the belt.

NOTE:

Work the first stitch of each row in the same stitch at the base of the beginning ch-2 (turning chain). After Round 1, the beginning ch-2 counts as 1 hdc.

Work the last stitch of each row into the top of the beginning ch-2 (into the second ch, counting from the bottom).

Work just into the front loop of the second turning ch if it's too hard to insert hook under both loops.

WING LAYERS

Using **black**, make a magic loop.

Round 1: ch 1 (not counted as a st), hdc 8 into magic loop (see Tutorials), skip the beginning ch 1, slst to top of first hdc to join, turn. (8 sts)

Continue in rows:

Row 2: change to **red**, ch 2 (count as first hdc here and throughout), hdc 1 in same stitch at base of beginning ch-2, [hdc-inc] 5 times, turn, leaving remaining stitches unworked. (12 sts)

Row 3: ch 2, hdc 1 in same st at base of beginning ch-2, [hdc 1, hdc-inc] 5 times, hdc 1, turn. (18 sts)

Row 4: ch 2, hdc in same st at base of beginning ch-2, [hdc 2, hdc-inc] 5 times, hdc 2, turn. (24 sts)

Row 5: ch 2, hdc in same st at base of beginning ch-2, [hdc 3, hdc-inc] 5 times, hdc 3, turn. (30 sts)

Row 6: ch 2, hdc in same st at base of beginning ch-2, hdc 4, hdc-inc, hdc 2, dc 2, [dc-inc, dc 4] twice, dc-inc, hdc 4, hdc-inc, hdc 4, turn. (36 sts)

Row 7: ch 1, sc 36.

Break yarn and fasten off.

Crochet another piece in the same way, using **off-white** throughout.

There are also yellow and black ladybirds with dots varying between 2 and 24. I hate them all!

1

2

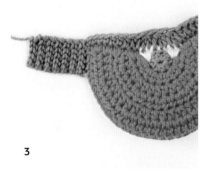

3

4

ASSEMBLING LAYERS

Take both parts of the wing suit. Hold the red piece at the front with the white one at the back. Insert hook into both corresponding stitches or spaces on both pieces to crochet them together:

Row 1: Join **red** yarn with a standing sc (see Tutorials), into the last stitch of Row 7 in the right corner of the flat end (counts as first sc), [sc-inc in the end of every second row] 4 times, change to **off-white**, °sc 3° in between the red row and the black circle, along the circle: skip 1, slstblo 1, skip 1, °sc 3° in between the red and black row, change to **red**, [sc-inc in the end of every second row] 4 times, sc 1 into the first stitch of Row 7 on the left corner (see photo 1). (24 sts)

Break yarn and fasten off.

Row 2: Join the **black** yarn (shown as grey in photos for clarity) with a standing sc into the first red stitch on the right corner of the flat end (counts as first sc), sc 3, hdc 4, [dc3tog] 3 times, hdc 4, sc 4 (see photo 2). (19 sts)

BELT

Rotate 90 degrees clockwise and crochet along the front of the wing suit, inserting the hook into the corresponding stitches on both wing layers to crochet them together as follows:

Row 1: ch 1 (counts as first st), sc 1 into the end of the red row, sc 3 across the stitches on the edge of the wing layers, turn. (5 sts)

Rows 2–14: ch 1, slstblo 5, turn (13 rows) (see photo 3).

Break the yarn with a long tail. Pull the tail through the last stitch completely and use it to sew the end of the 5 stitches on the opposite side of the wing suit (see photo 4). Weave in all ends.

DOTS (MAKE 3)

Using **black**, make a magic loop (see Tutorials).

Round 1: sc 13 into magic loop.

Break the yarn with a long tail, tighten the loop then fasten off invisibly into the first sc (see Tutorials). Use the remaining yarn tail to sew the dots onto the wing suit (see photo for placement).

STAG BEETLE (Lucanus cervus)

MATERIALS

HOOK SIZE: US C/2 (2.5mm or 2.25mm)

YARN: Scheepjes Catona 4ply (sport), 100% cotton, 25g/62m – 1 ball of each shade

- 130 Old Lace (off white)
- 162 Black Coffee (dark brown)
- 383 Ginger Gold (golden brown)
- 397 Cyan (light blue)
- 401 Dark Teal (emerald)

YOU ALSO NEED:

- Toy filling
- 5mm black toy safety eyes

PATTERN

HEAD

Using **off-white**, follow the top-down head pattern (see Basic Shapes: Head Pattern).

BODY

Using **golden brown**, follow the beetle larva body pattern (see Beetle Larva).

HAT

Using **dark brown**, follow the hat pattern with pointy beetle edge (see Basic Shapes: Hat Pattern).

WING SUIT

The wing suit is made by crocheting 2 separate wing layers, 1 in light blue/emerald and 1 in off-white. These are assembled into one piece before working the belt.

107

NOTE:

Work the first stitch of each row in the same stitch at the base of the beginning ch-2 (turning chain). After Round 1, the beginning ch-2 counts as 1 hdc.

Work the last stitch of each row into the top of the beginning ch-2 (this is the second ch, counting from the bottom).

Work just into the front loop of the second turning ch if it's too hard to insert hook under both loops.

1

WING LAYERS

Using **light blue**, make a magic loop (see Tutorials).

Round 1: ch 2 (not counted as st), hdc 6 into magic loop, turn. (6 sts)

Continue in rows:

Row 2: ch 2 (counts as first hdc here and throughout), hdc 1 in same st at base of beginning ch-2, [hdc-inc] 5 times, turn, leaving the top of the beginning ch-2 unworked. (12 sts)

Row 3: ch 2, hdc 1 in same st at base of beginning ch-2, [hdc 1, hdc-inc] 5 times, hdc 1, turn. (18 sts)

Row 4: ch2, hdc 1 in same st at base of beginning ch-2, [hdc 2, hdc-inc] 5 times, hdc 2, turn. (24 sts)

Row 5: ch 2, hdc 1 in same st at base of beginning ch-2, [hdc 3, hdc-inc] 5 times, hdc 3, turn. (30 sts)

Row 6: change to **emerald**, ch 2, hdc 1 in same st at base of beginning ch-2, hdc 4, hdc-inc, hdc 2, dc 2, [dc-inc, dc 4] twice, dc-inc, hdc 4, hdc-inc, hdc 4, turn. (36 sts)

Row 7: ch1, sc 36.

Break yarn and fasten off.

Crochet another piece in the same way, using **off-white** throughout.

ASSEMBLING LAYERS

Take both parts of the wing suit. Hold the blue piece at the front with the white one at the back. Insert hook into both corresponding stitches or spaces on both pieces to crochet them together.

Row 1: Join **dark brown** yarn with a standing sc (see Tutorials), into the last stitch of Row 7 in the right corner of the flat end (counts as first sc), [sc-inc in each end of every second row] 4 times, sc-inc into the initiating magic loop,

[sc-inc into the end of every second row] (4 times), sc 1 into the last stitch on the left corner, turn (see photo 1 where yarn is shown as grey for clarity). (20 sts)

Row 2: ch 1 (not counted as a st), slst 20, turn. (20 sts)

Row 3: ch 1, sc 3, hdc 4, [dc2tog] 3 times, hdc 4, sc 3. (17 sts)

BELT

Rotate 90 degrees clockwise, and crochet along the front of the wing suit. Insert hook through both corresponding stitches on both wing layers to crochet them together as follows:

Row 1: ch 1 (counts as first st), sc 4, turn. (5 sts)

Rows 2–15: ch 1, slstblo 5, turn (14 rows).

Break the yarn with a long tail. Pull the tail through the last stitch completely and use it to sew the end of the 5 stitches on the opposite side of the wing suit. Weave in all ends.

ANTLERS (MAKE 2)

Using **dark brown**, ch 9.

Row 1: starting in the 2nd back bump from hook: slst 2, sc 1, ch 5 (see photo 2), crochet into the bumps on the back of the ch-5 (see Tutorials): starting in the 2nd back bump from hook: slst 1, sc 2, hdc 1, °hdc 3° into the space underneath the post of the sc stitch (see photo 3), continue into the back bumps of original chain: hdc 1, dc 1, dc-inc, dc 2 (see photo 4).

Break the yarn with a long tail and fasten off.

Crochet a row of surface crochet slip stitches onto the front side of the right antler and the wrong side of the left antler (see photo 5 where stitches are shown in white for clarity).

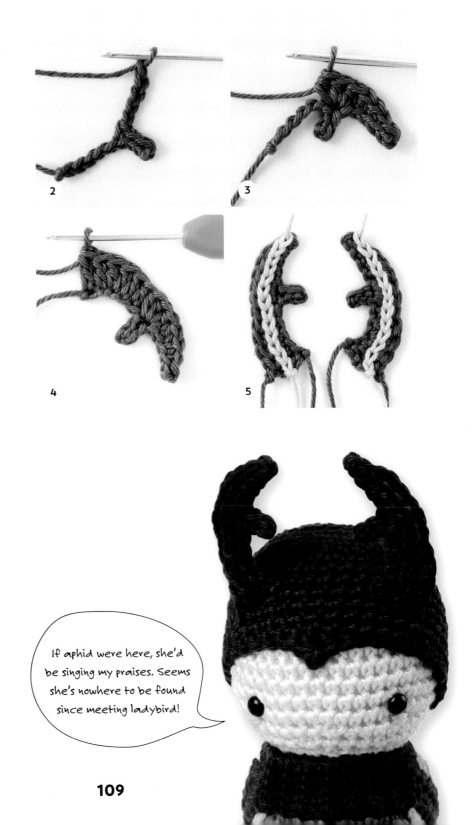

> **SURFACE CROCHET STITCHES**
>
> Put a slip knot from your yarn onto the hook. Insert hook in between the posts of the first two dc stitches on the bottom of the antler. Hold the working thread behind the fabric. Pull a loop of your working yarn through the space and the loop on your hook in the same way as a standard slip stitch, then repeat into every space between the posts of the stitches until you reach the tip of the antler.

FINISHING

ANTLERS

Place the antlers onto the hat, the inner corners in line with the 5th round from the hat's edge, with a distance of 6 stitches apart, outer corners in line with the 3rd round from the hat's edge. Sew the antlers onto the hat, using the remaining yarn tails.

> If aphid were here, she'd be singing my praises. Seems she's nowhere to be found since meeting ladybird!

FLY MAGGOT

MATERIALS

HOOK SIZE: US C/2 (2.5mm or 2.25mm)

YARN: Scheepjes Catona 4ply (sport), 100% cotton, 25g/62m – 1 ball of each shade
- 130 Old Lace (off white)
- 101 Candle Light (pale yellow)

YOU ALSO NEED:
- Toy filling
- 5mm black toy safety eyes

> Fruit flies were the first astronauts, reaching outer space aboard a US V-2 rocket in 1947.

PATTERN

HEAD

Using **off-white**, follow the top-down head pattern (see Basic Shapes: Head Pattern), ending after Round 17. Change to **pale yellow** in the last step of the last stitch on the head.

BODY

Round 18: slst 14.

Work all the following rounds only into the back loops of the stitches.

Round 19: scblo 14.

Round 20: [scblo 1, scblo-inc] 7 times. (21 sts)

Rounds 21–22: scblo 21 (2 rounds).

Round 23: scblo 1, scblo-inc, [scblo 2, scblo-inc] 6 times, scblo 1. (28 sts)

Rounds 24–26: scblo 28 (3 rounds).

Round 27: [sc2tog-blo, scblo 5] 4 times. (24 sts)

Round 28: scblo 2, sc2tog-blo, [scblo 4, sc2tog-blo] 3 times, scblo 2. (20 sts)

Stuff the body firmly.

Round 29: [sc2tog-blo, scblo 3] 4 times. (16 sts)

Round 30: scblo 1, sc2tog-blo, [scblo 2, sc2tog-blo] 3 times, scblo 1. (12 sts)

Round 31: [sc2tog-blo, scblo 1] 4 times. (8 sts)

Add more toy filling, break the yarn and close the round through the back loops (see Tutorials), then weave in all yarn tails.

HAT

Using **pale yellow**, follow the hat pattern with standard plain edge (see Basic Shapes: Hat Pattern).

FLY PUPA

MATERIALS

HOOK SIZE: US C/2 (2.5mm or 2.25mm)

YARN: Scheepjes Catona 4ply (sport), 100% cotton, 25g/62m

· 1 ball of Shade 388 Rust (red)

PATTERN

NOTE:

The beginning ch-3 is not counted as a stitch on any round.

Always work the first dcblo of each round into the next st along (after the joining slst).

CASE

Using **red**, make a magic loop (see Tutorials).

Round 1: ch 3 (not counted as a st here and throughout), dc 8 into magic loop, skip the beginning ch-3, slst to top of beginning ch-3. (8 sts)

Round 2: ch 3, dcblo-inc in every st, slst to top of beginning ch-3. (16 sts)

Round 3: ch 3, [dcblo 1, dcblo-inc] 8 times, slst to top of beginning ch-3. (24 sts)

Round 4: ch 3, [dcblo 2, dcblo-inc] 8 times, slst to top of beginning ch-3. (32 sts)

Round 5: ch 3, [dcblo 3, dcblo-inc] 8 times, slst to top of beginning ch-3. (40 sts)

Round 6: ch 3, dcblo 40, slst to top of beginning ch-3.

Round 7: ch 3, [dcblo 9, dcblo-inc] 4 times, slst to top of beginning ch-3. (44 sts)

Rounds 8–9: ch 3, dc 44, slst to top of beginning ch-3 (2 rounds).

Before you start the next round, count 7 dc stitches backwards and place a marker into the 7th dc stitch.

Round 10: ch 1, slst 7, ch 30, skip 30, take care not to twist the chain and slst 1 into marked stitch, slst 6, slst 1 into the beginning ch-1 to close the round.

Round 11: ch 3, dcblo 7, crochet into the back bumps on the back side of the chain (see Tutorials): dc 30, dcblo 7, slst to top of beginning ch-3.

Round 12: ch 3, dcblo 44, slst to top of beginning ch-3.

Round 13: ch 3, [dc2tog-blo, dcblo 9] 4 times, slst to top of beginning ch-3. (40 sts)

Round 14: ch 3, [dc2tog-blo, dcblo 3] 8 times, slst to top of beginning ch-3. (32 sts)

Round 15: ch 3, [dc2tog-blo, dcblo 2] 8 times, slst to top of beginning ch-3. (24 sts)

Round 16: ch 3, [dc2tog-blo, dcblo 1] 8 times, slst to top of beginning ch-3. (16 sts)

Round 17: ch 3, [dc2tog-blo] 8 times, slst to top of beginning ch-3. (8 sts)

Break the yarn and close remaining 8 stitches through the front loops (see Tutorials).

Ready for take off!

FLY (Lucilia sericata)

MATERIALS

HOOK SIZE: US C/2 (2.25mm or 2.5mm)

YARN: Scheepjes Catona 4ply (sport), 100% cotton, 25g/62m – 1 ball of each shade

- 130 Old Lace (off-white)
- 101 Candle Light (pale yellow)
- 401 Dark Teal (emerald)
- 390 Poppy Rose (red)
- 110 Jet Black (black)

YOU ALSO NEED:

- Toy filling
- 5mm black toy safety eyes

PATTERN

HEAD AND BODY

Using **off-white** and **pale yellow**, follow the pattern for the maggot (see Fly Maggot).

HAT

Using **emerald**, follow the hat pattern with standard plain edge (see Basic Shapes: Hat Pattern).

FLY EYES (MAKE 2)

Using **red**, make a magic loop (see Tutorials).

Round 1: sc 6 into magic loop. (6 sts)

Round 2: [sc-inc] 6 times. (12 sts)

Round 3: [sc 1, sc-inc] 6 times. (18 sts)

Round 4: sc 1, sc-inc, [sc 2, sc-inc] 5 times, sc 1. (24 sts)

Rounds 5–6: sc 24 (2 rounds).

Slst 1 into next st, break the yarn with a very long tail and close the round invisibly (see Tutorials).

ANTENNAE

Using **black**, follow type A antennae pattern (see Basic Shapes: Antennae).

WING SUIT

Using **emerald**, follow type B belt pattern (see Basic Shapes: Belt).

CLOSING THE BOTTOM OF THE BELT

The fly's wing suit fits on like a tiny sleeping bag, so now you need to work the bottom of the bag. Ch 1 then crochet along the edge, crocheting into the spaces between two ridges:

Round 1: [sc-inc in each space between two ridges] 12 times. (24 sts)

Rounds 2–3: hdcblo 24 (2 rounds).

Round 4: hdcblo 2, hdc2tog-blo, [hdcblo 4, hdc2tog-blo] 3 times, hdcblo 2. (20 sts)

Round 5: hdcblo 1, hdc2tog-blo, [hdcblo 2, hdc2tog-blo] 4 times, hdcblo 1. (15 sts)

Round 6: [sc2tog-blo, scblo 1] 5 times. (10 sts)

Break the yarn and close the remaining 10 stitches through the back loops (see Tutorials). Weave in all ends.

WINGS

WING PIECES (MAKE 4)

2 wing pieces made from the following pattern are joined to one wing in a second step.

Using **off-white**, ch 8.

Round 1: starting in the 2nd ch from hook, sc 2, hdc 2, dc 2, ch 3, [dc 1, ch 3] twice into the last ch, rotate and work into the remaining loops along the opposite side of the foundation chain: dc 2, hdc 2, sc 2. (14 sts + 3 ch-3 spaces)

Break the yarn and close invisibly into the 1st stitch of the round (see Tutorials). Weave in the ends on the wrong side.

JOINING 2 PIECES TO MAKE 1 WING

Hold two pieces with their wrong sides together (right sides are facing out). Crochet together the corresponding stitches or spaces along the edge of both pieces.

Join **off-white** with a standing sc (see Tutorials) into both the closing stitches on the tip of both pieces (counts as first st):

Round 1: sc 6, [sc 5 into the ch-3 sp] 3 times, sc 6, sc 1 into the closing stitch again. (29 sts)

Break the yarn with a long tail to sew the wing onto the suit and fasten off invisibly (see Tutorials) into the 1st stitch of the round.

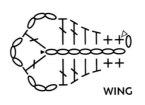

WING

ASSEMBLING

FLY EYES AND ANTENNAE

Use the long yarn tails to sew the fly eyes on the left side and the right side of the hat between the top of Round 3 (counting upwards from the rim) and the top of Round 3 (counting downwards from the middle of the magic loop on the top of the hat). Add a little bit of stuffing in between the fly eye and the hat to keep the shape, pin in position and sew (see Tutorials).

Sew the antennae onto the hat right above the 3rd round from the hat's edge, with a distance of 2 stitches between each antenna.

WINGS

Sew the wings with a few stitches left and right from the seam onto the back side of the suit (see photo).

113

SNAIL (Cepaea nemoralis)

MATERIALS:

HOOK SIZE: US C/2 (2.5mm or 2.25mm)

YARN: Scheepjes Catona 4ply (sport), 100% cotton, 25g/62m – 1 ball of each shade
- 130 Old Lace (off-white)
- 254 Moon Rock (light brown)
- 208 Yellow Gold (yellow)

YOU ALSO NEED:
- Toy filling
- 5mm black toy safety eyes

PATTERN

BODY

FRONT SIDE

Using **light brown**, ch 6.

Round 1: crochet into the bumps on the back of the chain (see Tutorials): starting in 2nd back bump from hook: sc 5 along the chain, turn. (5 sts)

Round 2: ch 1 (not counted as a stitch here and throughout), sc 5, turn.

Round 3: ch 1, sc-inc, sc 3, sc-inc, turn. (7 sts)

Round 4: ch 1, sc 7, turn.

Round 5: ch 1, sc-inc, sc 5, sc-inc, turn. (9 sts)

Rounds 6–10: ch 1, sc 9, turn (5 rounds).

Round 11: sc2tog, sc 5, sc2tog, turn. (7 sts)

Round 12: sc2tog, sc 3, sc2tog, turn. (5 sts)

Round 13: sc2tog, sc 1, sc2tog, turn. (3 sts)

Round 14: sc2tog, sc 1, turn. (2 sts)

Round 15: sc2tog. (1 st)

Break the yarn and fasten off.

BACK SIDE

Using **light brown**, ch 8.

Round 1: crochet into the bumps on the back of the chain (see Tutorials): starting in 2nd back bump from hook: sc 7 along the chain, turn. (7 sts)

Round 2: ch 1 (not counted as a stitch here and throughout), sc 7, turn. (7 sts)

Round 3: ch 1, sc 3, sc-inc, sc 3, turn. (8 sts)

Round 4: ch 1, sc 8, turn.

Round 5: ch 1, sc 3, [sc-inc] twice, sc 3, turn. (10 sts)

Round 6: ch 1, sc 10, turn.

Round 7: ch 1, sc 4, [sc-inc] twice, sc 4, turn. (12 sts)

Rounds 8–9: ch 1, sc 12, turn (2 rounds).

Round 10: ch 1, sc 4, [sc2tog] twice, sc 4, turn. (10 sts)

Round 11: ch 1, sc 3, [sc2tog] twice, sc 3, turn. (8 sts)

Round 12: ch 1, sc 2, [sc2tog] twice, sc 2, turn. (6 sts)

Round 13: sc 1, [sc2tog] twice, sc 1, turn. (4 sts)

Round 14: ch 1, [sc2tog] twice, turn. (2 sts)

Round 15: ch 1, sc2tog. (1 st)

Break the yarn and fasten off.

ASSEMBLING FRONT AND BACK

Hold together the front and the back layer so the stitches align, front piece is facing you, flat end points to the right, tip points to the left. Crochet the following row through the corresponding spaces at the end of the rows on both pieces to join them:

Join **light brown** with a standing sc (see Tutorials) into the space on the bottom of the first row, sc 13 along the spaces in between the ends of the rows until you reach the stitch on the tip, °sc 3° into the stitch on the tip, sc 14 along the other side of the body (see photo 1) until you reach the opposite side of the flat open end of the body (neck), ch 1, rotate 90 degrees clockwise, crochet along the stitches that remained from the foundation chain of the first row of the front side piece: sc 2 (place marker into the first sc – this stitch is where you go on with the head in the next round), sc-inc, sc 2. Turn the back facing you and crochet across the remaining foundation chain stitches of the back piece, sc 3, sc-inc, sc 3 (see photo 2). You now have 14 stitches along the neck to start the head. Stuff the body to define its shape.

HEAD

Using **off-white**, follow the bottom-up head pattern (see Basic Shapes: Head Pattern).

HAT

Using **light brown**, follow the hat pattern with standard plain edge (see Basic Shapes: Hat Pattern).

TENTACLES

Using **light brown**, make a magic loop (see Tutorials).

Round 1: sc 6 into magic loop. (6 sts)

Round 2: [sc-inc] 6 times. (12 sts)

Round 3: sc 12.

Round 4: [sc2tog] 6 times. (6 sts)

Stuff the sphere loosely.

Rounds 5–6: sc 6 (2 rounds).

Round 7: [sc-inc] 6 times. (6 sts)

Slst 1 into the 1st stitch of the round, break the yarn leaving a long rest to sew on the tentacle. Close the round invisibly (see Tutorials).

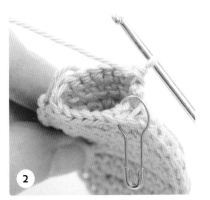

Pssst – you're naked!

Does that make me a slug?

SHELL

Using **yellow**, make a magic loop (see Tutorials).

Round 1: sc 7 into magic loop. (7 sts)

Round 2: [sc-inc] 7 times. (14 sts)

Round 3: [sc 1, sc-inc] 7 times. (21 sts)

Round 4: sc 1, sc-inc, [sc 2, sc-inc] 6 times, sc 1. (28 sts)

Round 5: [sc 3, sc-inc] 7 times. (35 sts)

Take the **yellow** loop off the hook and place it onto a stitch marker – you'll pick it up again later. From here onwards, alternate 2 colours whilst working in a spiral.

Join **off-white** yarn with a slip knot into the back loop of the first stitch of the next round (see Tutorials).

Round 6: ch 1, slstblo 34, take the off-white yarn loop off the hook and place it onto a stitch marker. (34 sts)

Round 7: pick up the **yellow** loop: slstblo 1 into the very first off-white chain stitch, scblol 1, hdcblo 1, dcblo 1, [dcblo-inc, dcblo 4] 6 times, dcblo-inc. (42 sts)

Round 8: take off **yellow** loop, pick up **off-white** loop: slst 42.

Round 9: take off **off-white** loop, pick up **yellow** loop: dcblo 42.

Round 10: take off **yellow** loop, pick up **off-white** loop: [skip 1, slst 1] 21 times. (21 sts)

Round 11: take off **off-white** loop, pick up **yellow** loop: [dcblo 1, dcblo-inc] 10 times, dcblo 1. (31 sts)

Round 12: take off **yellow** loop, pick up **off-white** loop: slst 1, [skip 1, slst 1] 15 times. (16 sts)

Round 13: take off **off-white** loop, pick up **yellow** loop: hdcblo 16.

Stuff the shell loosely with soft stuffing, just enough to make the shape stable.

Round 14: take off **yellow** loop, pick up **off-white** loop: [skip 1, slst 1] 8 times. (8 sts)

Round 15: take off **off-white** loop, pick up **yellow** loop: sc 8.

Add some more soft stuffing into the tip of the shell loosely.

Break the **off-white** yarn with a very long tail and pull the yarn tail through the last off-white loop completely. Break the **yellow** yarn and use the yellow yarn tail to close the last 8 yellow stitches through the front loops (see Tutorials), weave in end.

Thread the **off-white** yarn onto a tapestry needle. To make the last twist of the swirl, insert the needle into the centre of the just closed yellow stitches and then out next to where the yarn tail came from.

Turn the shell upside down and stitch through every remaining off-white front loop, as you do when you close remaining stitches (see photo 3). Pull the thread carefully every 5 stitches to tighten the stitches and define the shell shape even more.

Continue until the last off-white stitch. Do not tighten down the last two off-white rows on the bottom of the shell.

ASSEMBLING

SHELL

Place the shell onto the back of the body of the snail. The very first **off-white** stitch on the bottom of the shell should stand in a line with the tip of the body. Use some pins to keep the shell in place for sewing (see photos 4 and 5). Sew the shell onto the body using the same yarn as for the shell (**yellow**). Sew the shell onto the back side of the body through the remaining **yellow** front loops on the edge of the bottom of the shell.

TENTACLES

With the remaining yarn tails, sew the tentacles onto the hat (see Tutorials). The right position for the tentacles is between the top of Round 4 and the bottom of Round 9, counting upwards from the rim. The closest distance between the tentacles on height of Round 6 should be 3–4 stitches. When the hat is put on the head, the tentacles should stay in a vertical line with the eyes.

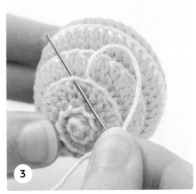

Snails and slugs are hermaphrodites, which means they are male and female at once.

APHID (Aphidoidea)

Nature made aphids in an impressive collection of different colours – green, yellow, orange, brown, black, white, red and even apricot. Choose whatever colour you like the most.

And finally, the most important bug of all … me!

MATERIALS:

HOOK SIZE: US C/2 (2.5mm or 2.25mm)

YARN: Scheepjes Catona 4ply (sport), 100% cotton, 25g/62m – 1 ball of each shade
· 205 Kiwi (lime green)
· 392 Lime Juice (light green)

YOU ALSO NEED:
· 5mm black toy safety eyes
· 3mm light green beads x 6 (optional)
· Beading thread
· Toy filling

PATTERN

BODY

Using **light green**, make a magic loop (see Tutorials).

Round 1: sc 5 into magic loop. (5 sts)

Round 2: sc-inc in every st. (10 sts)

Round 3: [sc 1, sc-inc] 5 times. (15 sts)

Round 4: sc 1, sc-inc, [sc 2, sc-inc] 4 times, sc 1. (20 sts)

Place the eyes between the 3rd and 4th rounds – the first eye into the bottom of the stitch before the 2nd increase in Round 4 and the second eye into the bottom of the stitch after the 4th increase in the same round.

Change to **lime green**.

Round 5: [scblo 3, scblo-inc] 5 times. (25 sts)

Round 6: sc 25.

Round 7: sc 2, sc-inc, [sc 4, sc-inc] 4 times, sc 2. (30 sts)

Rounds 8–10: sc 30 (3 rounds).

Round 11: [sc2tog, sc 3] 6 times. (24 sts)

Round 12: sc 24.

Round 13: sc 1, sc2tog, [sc 2, sc2tog] 5 times, sc 1. (18 sts)

Round 14: [sc2tog, sc 1] 6 times. (12 sts)

Stuff the body.

Round 15: [sc2tog] 6 times. (6 sts)

Stuff the body a bit more; break yarn and fasten off. Close the remaining stitches with the yarn tail, through front loops (see Tutorials). Weave in all yarn ends.

We've got a special relationship with ants. We produce honeydew for them and in return, they protect us from predators and other dangers. Just like farmers and their cattle!

FINISHING

ANTENNAE

Knot one end of a 10cm (4in) **light green** yarn piece and thread the other end onto a tapestry needle. Insert the needle through the body from the bottom side of the body towards one of the two stitches in the very centre of the forehead, right above the remaining light green front loops of Round 4. Make sure to stitch through the soft stuffing inside the body! Pull the yarn, so the knot slips through the fabric on the bottom side of the body and can't be seen anymore. On the aphid's head make another knot into the yarn thread at the height of approx. 2cm (1in). Cut the yarn above the knot. Make a second antenna the same way into the 2nd stitch on the centre of the forehead.

FEET

THREAD LEGS

Knot one end of a 10cm (4in) dark green yarn piece and thread the other end onto a tapestry needle. Insert the needle into the base of the body, taking it through the stuffing and out to the other side through the stitch you want to place the first leg at (see photo 1 for position); pull the yarn so the knot slips into the fabric so it is secured. On the other side of the

body, make another knot into the yarn thread at the height of approx. 1cm (½in). Cut the yarn above the knot. Repeat until you've made all 6 feet, taking care to pair them up at each side.

BEAD FEET

Sew 3 beads to each side of the body. They should stand in a line, the first foot in a stitch between the 1st and the 2nd lime green body round. Place the second and third foot each one round above the other (see photo 1).

Knot one end of a long piece of beading (or invisible) thread and thread the other end onto a tapestry needle. Stitch through the body (and the soft stuffing) all the way to the opposite side and come out through the stitch where you want to place the first foot. Pull a little, so the knot slips inside the body. Pull the thread through a 3mm bead and stitch back into the same stitch to come out one stitch along in the next row. Repeat as for the first foot until all 3 feet are sewn on in a line (see photo 2). Then, stitch all the way through the body to come out at the stitch where you want to place the first bead foot on the other side; stitch the remaining 3 beads in the same way to make 3 pairs of feet.

BLUSH

Embroider a little blush underneath the eyes using a thread of pink coloured yarn.

VENUS FLYTRAP (Dionaea muscicapa)

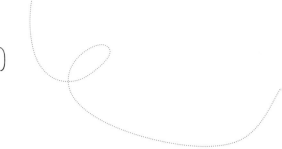

The main version of this extraordinary plant is made with a purse frame that closes with a satisfying snap, but instructions have also been given for an alternative zip version.

MATERIALS:

HOOK SIZE: US E/4 (3.5mm)

YARN: Scheepjes Stone Washed XL (worsted), 70% cotton, 30% acrylic 50g/75m – 1 ball of each shade

· 859 New Jade (pale green)
· 847 Red Jasper (red)
· 856 Coral (orange)

YOU ALSO NEED:

· Gold metallic effect sewing or embroidery thread (Rico Design Metallic No. 40 in Shade 941 Gold) (optional)
· Strong nylon thread
· Purse frame, half circle 20 x 10.5cm (8 x 4⅛in) ('Rebecca' by Prym) or 30cm (12in) zip

PATTERN

The Venus flytrap is made from 2 circle layers: an outer layer made from **pale green** held with **metallic thread** and an inner layer made from **red** and **orange**.

> **NOTE:**
>
> The beginning 3-ch counts as first dc.
>
> After the 2nd round the first dc of a new round is worked into the next stitch along, after the beginning 3-ch.

OUTSIDE LAYER

Using **pale green** and **metallic thread** held together, make a magic loop (see Tutorials).

Round 1: ch 3 (counts as first dc here and throughout), dc 11 into magic loop, slst to top of beginning ch-3. (12 sts)

Round 2: ch 3, dc in same st at base of ch-3, [dc-inc] 11 times, slst to top of beginning ch-3. (24 sts)

From now on, start the round by working into the next stitch along, after the beginning ch-3.

The flytrap is one of the fastest plants on earth.

Round 3: ch 3, dc-inc, [dc 1, dc-inc] 11 times, slst to top of beginning ch-3. (36 sts)

Round 4: ch 3, dc 1, dc-inc, [dc 2, dc-inc] 11 times, slst to top of beginning ch-3. (48 sts)

Round 5: ch 3, dc 2, dc-inc, [dc 3, dc-inc] 11 times, slst to top of beginning ch-3. (60 sts)

Round 6: ch 3, dc 3, dc-inc, [dc 4, dc-inc] 11 times, slst to top of beginning ch-3. (72 sts)

Round 7: ch 3, dc 4, dc-inc, [dc 5, dc-inc] 11 times, slst to top of beginning ch-3. (84 sts)

Round 8: ch 3, dc 5, dc-inc, [dc 6, dc-inc] 11 times. (96 sts)

Break the yarn and close the round invisibly into the top of the first dc (see Tutorials).

Weave in all ends on the wrong side of the fabric.

INSIDE LAYER

Using **red** and referring to the note, make a magic loop and follow Rounds 1–6 as given for the outside layer.

Round 7: ch 3, dc 4, dc-inc, [dc 5, dc-inc] 11 times. (84 sts)

NOTE:

Try to crochet the stitches for the inside layer a little bit tighter than the first circle, to create an inner layer that's slightly smaller than the pale green outer layer. If that doesn't work for you, crochet the last round (Round 8) using hdc stitches instead of dc stitches.

Break the yarn and close the round invisibly into the top of the first dc.

Join **orange** with a slip knot into the closing stitch.

Round 8: ch 3, dc 5, dc-inc, [dc 6, dc-inc] 11 times. (96 sts)

Break the yarn and close the round invisibly into the top of the first dc.

Weave in all ends on the wrong side of the fabric.

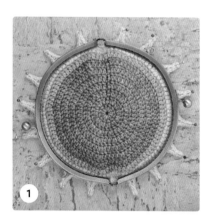

JOINING THE CIRCLES TO 1 PIECE (FOR PURSE FRAME VERSION)

Lay both circles flat on top of each other, right sides outside. The pale green layer is uppermost, the red circle is at the back.

To join both layers into one, insert the hook through the corresponding stitches on both layers and crochet them together with the following round:

Hold together **pale green** and **metallic thread** and join them with a slip knot into the closing stitches of both layers.

Round 9: ch 3, dc 6, dc-inc, [dc 7, dc-inc] 11 times. (108 sts)

Break the yarn and close the round invisibly into the top of the first dc (see Tutorials). Weave in all ends.

TEETH BORDER

Turn the piece so the orange layer is facing, then join **pale green** and **metallic thread** with a slip knot into the closing stitch of the last round.

Round 10: [slst 5, ch 5, work into the bumps on the back of the chain (see Tutorials), start in the 2nd back bump from hook: slst 2, sc 2, skip 1 on the edge of the circle] 8 times, slst 6, [slst 5, ch 5, work into the bumps on the back of the chain, start in the 2nd back bump from hook: slst 2, sc 2, skip 1 on the edge of the circle] 8 times, slst 5.

Break the yarn and close invisibly into the first slst. Weave in all ends.

FINISHING

SEWING IN THE PURSE FRAME

Using strong nylon thread, sew the edge of the circle to the purse frame. Sew around the posts of the stitches of Round 9.

BLOCKING

To keep the teeth standing straight up, block them after sewing the layers onto the purse frame (see photo 1). Open the frame flat and lay it down with its outside underneath and the inside uppermost. Stretch the teeth out and fix each tooth in position with a pin. Spray the teeth with water and leave to dry completely.

ALTERNATIVE VERSION WITH ZIP

For the zip version, the circle layers are joined together by sewing the zip in between them, so crochet Round 9 onto each single circle layer. Then lay both circles flat on top of each other, right sides outside. Sew the zip in between the two layers along the edge of the circles. After sewing, crochet the teeth border (Round 10) into the stitches of the last round of the outside layer.

LEAF

MATERIALS:

HOOK SIZE: US E/4 or
US G/6 (3.5mm or 4mm)

YARN: Scheepjes Stone
Washed XL (worsted), 70%
cotton, 30% acrylic 50g/75m

· 1 ball of Shade 846 Canada
  Jade (green)

**OTHER RECOMMENDED
COLOUR SHADES:**

· 859 New Jade (pale green)
· 852 Lemon Quartz (yellow)
· 849 Yellow Jasper (mustard)
· 856 Coral (orange)

YOU ALSO NEED:

· 20mm wooden bead or
  button (optional)

NOTE:

After the 2nd round the first dc of a
new round is worked into the next
stitch along, after the beginning
3-ch.

Always close the round with a slst
into the top of the beginning ch-3
chain.

PATTERN

Using **green** or chosen colour, make a
magic loop (see Tutorials).

Round 1: ch 3 (counts as first dc here
and throughout), dc 13 into magic loop
(see Tutorials), slst to top of beginning
ch-3. (14 sts)

Round 2: ch 3, dc in same st at base of
ch-3, [dc-inc] 3 times, [tr-inc] 6 times,
[dc-inc] 4 times, slst to top of beginning
ch-3. (28 sts)

From now on, start the round by working
into the next stitch along, after the
beginning ch-3.

Round 3: ch 3, [dc-inc, dc 1] 5 times,
[tr-inc, tr 1] 3 times, tr-inc, [dc 1, dc-inc]
5 times, slst to top of beginning ch-3.
(42 sts)

Round 4: ch 3, dc 1, dc-inc, [dc 2, dc-inc]
4 times, dc 2, tr-inc, [tr 2, tr-inc] 3 times,
[dc 2, dc-inc] 5 times, slst to top of
beginning ch-3. (56 sts)

Round 5: ch 3, dc 2, dc-inc, [dc 3, dc-inc]
4 times, dc 3, [tr-inc, tr 3] 2 times, tr-inc,
[dc 3, dc-inc] 6 times, slst to top of
beginning ch-3. (70 sts)

Round 6: ch 3, dc 3, dc-inc, [dc 4, dc-inc]
3 times, dc 2; **first bite:** °dc 1 + ch 2 +

sc 1°, °sc 1 + ch 2 + slst 1°, slst 2, °sc 1 +
ch 2 + sc 1°, sc 1, °sc 1 + ch 2 + dc 1°, dc 3,
°dc 1 + tr 1°, tr 2, °tr 1 + ch2picot + tr 1°,
tr 2, °tr 1 + dc 1°, [dc 4, dc-inc] 3 times,
dc 3; **second bite:** °dc 1 + ch 2 + sc 1°,
sc 2, ch 2, slst 4, °sc 1 + ch 2 + dc 1°,
dc 4, dc-inc, slst to top of beginning
ch-3 (87 sts, not including ch 2 and
ch2picot); continue with the **stem:**
ch 13, slst into the same stitch on the
base of the ch-13 chain.

Break the yarn and fasten off invisibly
(see Tutorials).

FINISHING

Weave in the end on the wrong side of
the leaf.

Sew the bead or button onto the front
side of the leaf at its tip, in between
Rounds 5 and 6.

Now you can wrap your caterpillar and
her egg into the leaf and close it with
the button and the stem loop.

ABOUT THE AUTHOR

Hi, I'm Lydia!

I'm a crochet enthusiast, notorious yarn buyer and snail shell collector (just one of my numerous obsessions). I'm also chief of the lalylala amigurumi tribe and one of my most impressive skills is to crochet while walking.

My biggest inspiration is my little boy, who's also my most selective toy and story tester. He continuously brings me back to the magic that happens in the smallest things in our everyday life.

I'm also a lucky beggar to have a man on my side who's not just my most patient supporter, but also wrote the wonderful story for the book you are holding in your hands. Plus, he's also the world's one and only theoretical crochet expert without any practical experience.

Working with yarn is the red thread through my life. It's unlikely that you would meet me without a survival bag full of yarn and hooks. My great grandma taught me how to crochet when I was a child. After a short crafting break during my teenage years, I picked up the red thread again with the same childlike joy. I moved to Lalylaland and made a lot of friends there. Most of them are weirdos wearing animal costumes, but I like them!

Come and join us for a cup of coffee and a little crochet at www.lalylala.com.

 facebook.com/lalylala.handmade

 instagram.com/lalylaland

ACKNOWLEDGMENTS

First of all, I thank YOU, my dear lalylala crochet friend! Without your unshakable crochet enthusiasm and support, I should never have been able to make a book project like this!

To make a book, it needs a publishing house to believe in the author and the idea.

I'd like to thank the lovely team at F&W Media International:

Sarah Callard and Jeni Hennah for the perfect preparation and coordination of the project and the entire team. Cheryl Brown, for her incredible ability to connect all the loose ends to a well arranged book. Anna Wade, for her creative ideas, the charming design of the book and her endless patience with all my interventions. Prudence Rogers, for bringing the bugs to life with her magical and wonderful illustrations. Lynne Rowe, for the professional tracking of all the small and bigger 'bugs' during the pattern checking.

For the generously provided Scheepjes wool, I thank Eddy Koelewijn of DeBondt.

And finally, from the bottom of my heart, I give a hug to my family and friends for their praise, critique, encouragement and love. Katja, for your help with the English translation and for giving the details of the story the final twist. And above all: Mischa – the great chronicler of the adventure of our crocheted insect friends – not only for your imagination and serenity, but also for countless toddler activity hours and non-stop supply of coffee!

SUPPLIERS

For Scheepjes yarn:

UK

DERAMORES

www.deramores.com

WOOL WAREHOUSE

www.woolwarehouse.co.uk

LOOP

www.loopknitting.com

BLACK SHEEP WOOLS

www.blacksheepwools.com

US

PARADISE FIBERS

www.paradisefibers.com

AMERICA'S YARN STORE

www.yarn.com

WORLDWIDE

ETSY

www.etsy.com

For metallic thread, zips, beads, buttons and Prym products:

SEWANDSO

www.sewandso.co.uk

HOBBYCRAFT

www.hobbycraft.co.uk

JO ANN FABRIC & CRAFT STORES

www.joann.com

HOBBY LOBBY

www.hobbylobby.com

JOHN LEWIS

www.johnlewis.com

INDEX

A SEWANDSO BOOK
© F&W Media International, Ltd 2017

SewandSo is an imprint of F&W Media International, Ltd
Pynes Hill Court, Pynes Hill, Exeter, EX2 5AZ, UK

F&W Media International, Ltd is a subsidiary of F+W Media, Inc
10151 Carver Road, Suite #200, Blue Ash, OH 45242, USA

Text and Designs © Lydia Tresselt 2017
Layout and Photography © F&W Media International, Ltd 2017

First published in the UK and USA in 2017

A catalogue record for this book is available from the British Library.

ISBN-13: 978-1-4463-0666-6 hardback
SRN: R5830 hardback

ISBN-13: 978-1-4463-7631-7 PDF
SRN: R5882 PDF

ISBN-13: 978-1-4463-7632-4 EPUB
SRN: R5881 EPUB

Printed in China by RR Donnelley for:
F&W Media International, Ltd
Pynes Hill Court, Pynes Hill, Exeter, EX2 5AZ, UK

10 9 8 7 6 5 4 3 2 1

Content Director: Ame Verso
Acquisitions Editor: Sarah Callard
Senior Editor: Jeni Hennah
Project Editor: Cheryl Brown
Proofreader: Jane Trollope
Design Manager: Anna Wade
Designer: Sarah Rowntree
Art Direction and Illustration: Prudence Rogers
Photographer: Jason Jenkins
Production Manager: Beverley Richardson

F&W Media publishes high quality books on a wide range of subjects.
For more great book ideas visit: www.sewandso.co.uk

Layout of the digital edition of this book may vary depending on reader hardware and display settings.

Where crafters come to shop...

Find everything you need for your next craft project amongst thousands of products in needlecraft, sewing, knitting and more.

INTERNATIONAL
SHIPPING

NEXT-DAY
DELIVERY

DEDICATED
CUSTOMER
SERVICES TEAM

EARN LOYALTY
POINTS AS
YOU SHOP

www.**sewandso**.co.uk